WOMEN
AT
WAR

VOICES FROM THE TWENTIETH CENTURY

EYEWITNESS ACCOUNTS FROM THE IMPERIAL WAR MUSEUM SOUND ARCHIVE

WOMEN AT WAR

CONSULTING EDITOR:
NIGEL FOUNTAIN

First published in Great Britain in 2002 by
Michael O'Mara Books Limited
9 Lion Yard, Tremadoc Road
London SW4 7NQ

A CIP catalogue record for this book is available from the British Library

ISBN 1-85479-857-X

1 3 5 7 9 10 8 6 4 2

Designed and typeset by Design 23

www.mombooks.com

Printed and bound in Singapore by Tien Wah Press

Cover images: background – IWM: PST 5184; foreground right – IWM: Q31011

This book has been produced with the co-operation and assistance of the Imperial War Museum, London, Britain's museum of national conflict. In particular, the consulting editor and the publishers wish to express their gratitude to the following members of the Museum's staff, for their help in preparing the text and illustrations:

Laurie Milner, senior historian with the Research and Information Department, and General Editor of the 'Voices From the Twentieth Century' series, whose idea the series was;

Margaret Brooks, Keeper of the Sound Archive, for her advice, encouragement and generous assistance over reproduction charges;

Dr Brad King, Keeper of the Department of Photographs, for generously granting permission to reproduce the Museum's images free of charge, and to the staff of the Department for their help in preparing prints;

Dr Christopher Dowling, OBE, Director of Public Services, and Elizabeth Bowers, Publications Officer, for their interest in the initial idea and for helping to bring about the Museum's involvement;

Barbara Levy, the Museum's literary agent, for her patient assistance in bringing that involvement to fruition.

Thanks also to Lynne Woolmer of River Records for providing music for the CD.

With the exception of IWM: PST 0759 (p.2) all images provided by the Imperial War Museum are credited in brackets following each caption. The remaining images are credited as follows:
Mary Evans Picture Library – pp. 10 (both), 11, 16 (below right), 17, 35, 38 (below right), 62 (right), 63, 66, 67, 74, 75 (above), 78 (both), 82, 93, 94, 99 (below right), 130, 133, 140, 141. **Mary Evans / Fawcett Library** – p. 18. **Mary Evans / The Women's Library** – p.62 (left). **Mary Evans / Explorer** – p. 86 (above). **Hulton Archive** – pp. 19 (both), 26, 27, 29, 30, 38 (above left), 40, 41, 44, 45, 46, 47 (above), 57, 58, 61, 64, 65, 69, 72, 73, 76-7, 91, 101, 119, 121, 124, 129, 132, endpapers. **TRH / R Winslade** – p.123.

CONTENTS

Author Acknowledgements

It was Toby Buchan and Gabrielle Mander at Michael O'Mara Books who crystallized the idea of this project. Together with their colleague Helen Cumberbatch, they provided the support and enthusiasm which saw it through. Picture editor Jackum Brown, and Judith Palmer, drew many of the spectacular images from the Imperial War Museum, and Ron Callow and Simon Buchanan of Design 23 put them together with the words.

Unfailingly helpful, staff at the IWM's Sound Archive, the keeper of the archive Margaret Brooks, Richard McDonough and John Stopford-Pickering, opened up the past to me – and John showed me routes through. Margaret, together with senior interviewer Conrad Wood and the rest of that group of IWM interviewers are the people who have created a priceless insight into the history of the twentieth century.

Encouragement, and forbearance came from Monica Henriquez as I worked on the project, and Sheila Rowbotham provided material, advice and insight. Without John Fordham's assistance much of the material would never have made it from transcript into computer, let alone book and CD. In Manchester the professionalism of Mike Thornton of One Stop Digital and producer Bob Dickinson made putting together the CD a pleasure.

Without the interviewees, there would have been no project. Without their extraordinary generation, the world would have been a very different, and much worse place.

INTRODUCTION

'Will ye go to Flanders?' the Scots sang in the seventeenth century. 'You'll see the bullets fly, and you'll hear the ladies cry. And the sodjers how they die.' In twentieth-century Flanders, and its equivalents around the world, soldiers were to die in their hundreds of thousands – but the ladies did far more than just cry, if they even had time to cry, many of them.

The words and voices of the women in *Women at War* come from people whose lives, taken together, cross three centuries. There are women who, as children of the British Empire shared the nineteenth-century planet with Queen Victoria and Oscar Wilde, and women who share the new millennium with Queen Elizabeth II and Madonna. But at the centre of all these lives are the two cataclysms of the first half of the twentieth century, Europe's two-part civil war: the Great War of 1914–18 and the Second World War of 1939–45. These were events so terrible that they shaped the century, and were still casting shadows on children born at the century's end.

Women of course have always been in wars – as warriors, camp followers, lovers, casualties, carers, protesters, instigators and victims. But war in the twentieth century was quite different. Industrialized war was an insatiable metal monster, consuming money, lives, empires; shaping the very structure of societies so that they could feed

Women test valves at the Royal Navy barracks, Portsmouth, in a painting by Arthur McCormick, 1916

The refuge worked: coming out of an Anderson shelter. (IWM: HU 635)

helped save the world.

Alongside cenotaphs and village war memorials, the Unknown Warrior, some mother's son, became a symbol of sacrifice, and of carnage. But alongside him is the unknown nurse, civil servant, munitions worker, ambulance driver, housewife, conscientious objector, cook, special agent, gunner, lover, war correspondent, officer, administrator, doctor – and, in their millions, the unknown relatives.

Women at War is not a history. Listening to the voices of these ordinary yet extraordinary women at the Imperial War Museum, and, I hope, reading their accounts here, is to embark on a form of time travel; but the country to be visited is vast, unimaginable. So what *Women at War* seeks to do, in focusing on a few women's voices, almost all British, is to catch fleeting experience. Some of these stories may echo in the lives of others; most will not, but they are messages from that land: the passing of Edward VII and a (false) sense of security; an English nurse's response to horrors of the Eastern Front of the First World War; apricots in a basket in Boulogne on a misty September morning in 1917; being thrown on the dole in the land fit for heroes; getting expelled for honesty from a German school in 1935; witnessing defeated Spanish Republican soldiers sprawled on the beaches of southern France a month before the Second World War erupts; being five and getting booed in High Wycombe in 1940, bombed in the Home Counties, jailed in Manchester – and entertained beyond the roof of the world.

Listening to these voices, reading the words, is an antidote to some stock assumptions about the past. In these wars, alongside danger, greyness, deprivation and bereavement there was also freedom, escape, and sisterhood. Edwardian England was not

it more effectively. Old cities went up in flames; and so did old ways, including the petty and not so petty restrictions that had confined women – the vote was to arrive, even if equal pay did not. The British Commonwealth nurses tending the trenches of 1916 were welcomed in France because they were schooled in new ways, unlike many of their French counterparts – nuns who were lost in this new era of big pushes and man-made seas of mud. A quarter of a century later the Women's Auxiliary Air Force plotters, radar operators, observers and monitors of the Battle of Britain worked at the frontier of global technology, and thus a lost paradise of long summer evenings and long dresses – there was something of that, true, but there was also gut-wrenching poverty, ever-present flies and incurable disease; unemployment for women from poor backgrounds, and indolence for the rich. The work of women constructing high-explosive and poison-gas shells – and beginning the chain which led to the horror of the trenches – was for many, at the time, blessed release from poverty. Conversely, the romance of the Blitz came after the event, the reality was sleepless nights, fear – and wet feet.

In those two wars, however, the state offered to women who had been nowhere, the chance to go, if not anywhere, then at least to the big city, and to some maybe the chance to go across the world; it offered to pay women more than many of them had ever earned in their lives. Suddenly welfare, decent wages, kindergartens, pie in the peacetime sky, became the aim – and sometimes reality – for wartime governments. Now, why could that be?

Conversational repetitions have been generally edited out, and some material composited, but, to the best of my ability, what is seen and heard is what was said by members of an heroic generation to the Museum's inspired and diligent questioners.

Female firefighters on standby at Millbay Fire station in Plymouth in 1942.

CHAPTER ONE

AUGUST 1914:
MY COUNTRY 'TIS OF THEE

IN 1914 **RUBY ORD** WAS EIGHTEEN, DOING statistical work, and living near Nottingham. Ruby was a patriot.

Britain before the First World War was still marvellous. Just to be British — it didn't matter how poor you were, unimportant in your own country, you were important in the world: you were a Briton. Only the people who lived in those days have any idea what it was like. At school on Empire Day we had the most gorgeous affairs, and everything was so different that when the war came we were fantastically patriotic. Not emotional in any other sense except for the sake of the country: it must be saved at all costs. What we stood for, everything we believed in was threatened.

In the world that was, wars were little, or seemed so, and far away. Closer to home there was the campaign for women's suffrage,

It seemed so easy: a British postcard of 1914.

Emmeline Pankhurst, leading British suffragist, founder of the Women's Social and Political Union (WSPU) in 1903.

There's life in the old Dog yet !

The funeral procession of King Edward VII, as witnessed by Antonia Gamwell in 1910.

industrial conflict, gut-wrenching poverty, the battle for Irish Home Rule. There were also chances for the crowned heads of Europe to meet, compare splendid uniforms and dazzling gowns, strut the world stage, before almost every one of them was swept away.

In 1910 **Antonia Gamwell**, a businessman's daughter, was nineteen, just out of Roedean public school. For her those were times for tours, often to Germany, and she even encountered the Kaiser. In May that year,

she stayed in Lowndes Square in Knightsbridge. From this grand address she was able to watch the funeral procession, from Westminster Hall to Paddington Railway Station, and then on to Windsor, of Edward VII, King of Great Britain and Ireland and of the British Dominions Beyond the Seas, and Emperor of India.

I was particularly pleased to do that because my uncle was walking with the coffin. Marching. We had a wonderful day. It was a magnificent procession, the last time that so many crowned heads came over to England, or were gathered together.

Alice Remington was the daughter of an architect and living in a village in North

Lancashire. In 1914 she was fifteen.

My mother was a clergyman's daughter and my father was a clergyman's son and they went to church twice on Sunday. They were very good citizens, they just stayed peacefully at home and read their Bible. My mother kept a beautiful larder with all the jams and the pickles. She saw that all was cleaned. She did an enormous amount of very beautiful embroidery, and she had her visiting days. I just got too bored with it for anything.

Within the lower depths were women like **Jane Cox**, thirteen years old in 1914, and living in East London's Mile End.

Women were dependent on their husbands. The only way they'd earn a shilling or two was to take in mangling, three halfpence a dozen, or do somebody's washing or go and scrub doorsteps or look after them in a confinement. We were in a very poor way, I've sat and watched other people eating, waited till they left a few crumbs, to eat what they'd leave.

Day in: in 1914 jobs for working-class women usually meant domestic service, laundry and low pay.
(IWM: Q 107058)

Margaret Warren was from Surrey.

It was an absolutely wonderful life, all parties, all fun, all dances, and for two years, nearly, we really had a gay life – everybody did. There was a sort of an idea of war, and people began thinking, should they do something; we used to have tennis parties and discuss what we could do, if we had to do anything, and I had an idea that I would do nothing except nurse. We none of us did anything at all, because there was no necessity. Then as time went on I realized that there would be a war, and so I went to various lectures and took the first aid course and the home nursing course. My mother said, 'Now, whatever you do, you're not going to nurse; I'm not going to have you nursing. You can go as a pantry-maid, yes, but not as a nurse.'

28 JUNE The Archduke Franz-Ferdinand, heir to the throne of Austria-Hungary, and his wife assassinated in Sarajevo, Serbia, by Gavrilo Princip, a young Bosnian member of the Greater Serbian Party

28 JULY Austria-Hungary declares war on Serbia

30 JULY Russia mobilizes in defence of Serbia

31 JULY Germany urges Russia to demobilize

Day out: middle-class women had leisure, but few career options.
(IWM: Q 107037)

Isabella Clarke was a Roman Catholic living in Belfast.

There wasn't much of a chance in Belfast to get a decent job. My mother was left a widow with the three of us. She only had half a crown a week from the Church to keep us.

Twenty-four-year-old **Mary Rumney** was a lawyer's daughter from the Potteries.

For we young women whose parents had sufficient money it was a test of endurance. You had arrived back, educated to the last hair, with nothing whatever to do. The servants did the housework, my mother did the management, and there was nothing except private dances, which were got up by the families round about.

There were war scares – in the press, in sensationalist books, feeding on diplomatic incidents like the 1911 Agadir crisis, when the Germans and French had clashed over their interests in Morocco. In 1914 **Agnes Allan** was living in Dundee.

We expected a German invasion. When my husband and I were in London, there was a play on and it was in two parts and one is, the Germans invaded England and all the people were in civilian clothes and they were all taken prisoner and shot. And then the next thing, the men were in Territorial Army uniform and the girls were in VAD uniform and they didn't get shot. That's all I remember about it.

War was not universally expected. At the age of nineteen, Buckinghamshire-born **Florence Farmborough** became a governess in Austria. Two years later, she had moved on to work in Kiev. She was twenty-seven in 1914.

Nearly every summer after I returned home from

I AUGUST Germany declares war on Russia

2 AUGUST German troops invade Luxembourg and Poland; Germany demands the right to violate Belgian territory, allegedly to defend against a French attack

3 AUGUST Belgium refuses German demands and appeals to Britain to safeguard Belgian sovereignty; Germany declares war on France; Britain prepares for general mobilization

1914

England, or before I went home to England, we would have a month in the country house – or dacha – of my friends. And I have been in many many country houses surrounded by the glorious forests and the glorious wide beautiful views, very often with hills and rivers of countryside in Russia. And always I have loved it.

But most of all I used to love the evenings when the young people would collect in the villages and would sing and would dance at night. And invariably the accordion would be played because someone in the village, someone always, could play the accordion. And around that person who played would be dancing and singing, the young folk of the village. From my window in the Ousov dacha I loved to listen to them. We just rejoiced in peace and freedom. We were supremely happy.

In 1913, encouraged by friends, **Eleanora Pemberton** had joined the Red Cross in the City of London.

We had no idea that there was going to be a European war. In 1913 my brother was working in Germany, got engaged and was eventually married. In July 1914 he and his wife, and the baby, and an English nurse, and their furniture, all went out to Hamburg. Well, that's to my mind conclusive proof that nobody was expecting war. He was interned of course.

Helen Pease was a child of what she called the 'ruling class of a ruling country', the daughter of a Liberal and later Labour MP. In 1914 she had just finished her first year at Newnham College Cambridge. On 28 June 1914, in Sarajevo, Bosnia, Archduke Franz Ferdinand, heir to the Emperor of Austria-Hungary and kingdom of Hungary, was assassinated by a Serb nationalist student,

A maid carries out duties for a wealthy family during wartime. (IWM: Q 107054)

4 AUGUST Formal British protest at Germany's violation of Belgian territory; Germany declares war on Belgium; British mobilization orders issued; British ultimatum to Germany is rejected; Britain declares war at 2300 hours

5 SEPTEMBER Britain, France and Russia pledge to make no separate peace with the Central Powers or their allies

Poster advertising the Red Cross. Many women joined the Red Cross as drivers or nurses in the Voluntary Aid Detachment (VAD).

Red Cross
Christmas
Roll Call
Dec. 16–23rd

The
GREATEST MOTHER
in the WORLD

6 AUGUST National Union of Women's Suffrage Societies (NUWSS) announces suspension of all political activity until the war ends. Women's Social and Political Union (WSPU) begins negotiating with the government which, on 10 August, announces the release of all imprisoned suffragettes; the WSPU agrees to end militant activities and help the war effort. The Women's Freedom League (WFL) disagrees, continuing its campaign for the vote

Archduke Franz Ferdinand (pictured with his wife and children), whose assassination precipitated the outbreak of war in Europe in August 1914. (IWM: Q 81810)

The arrest of Gavrilo Princip, the Serb nationalist student responsible for the assassination of Archduke Franz Ferdinand.

Gavrilo Princip. **Helen Pease** was home in the Potteries for the summer vacation.

> I was sticking my pressed flowers and sorting – I was doing botany – and Jessie Whitehead, that's the daughter of the mathematician, who was up with me, came in and said, 'The Archduke of Austria's been assassinated in Serbia. That means we shall have a war.'
>
> And I said, 'Oh, pooh, rubbish. What's Serbia got to do with us?'

1914 On the outbreak of war, two members of the WPSU, Dr Louisa Garrett Anderson and Dr Flora Murray, establish the Women's Hospital Corps. The War Office refuses to accept the services of women surgeons at the front and they are forced to work with the French Red Cross. The Women's Hospital Corps establishes hospitals in Paris and near Boulogne. Eventually the War Office gives permission for Garrett Anderson and Murray to establish the Women's Military Hospital in Endell Street, London

On 23 July Austria-Hungary sent Serbia an ultimatum. On 30 July the Russian Empire, backing its fellow Slavs, moved towards general mobilization. The German Empire issued an ultimatum against the Russians, demanding they stop mobilization, which the Russians refused. On 31 July the International Woman Suffrage Alliance, founded twelve years earlier, circulated its International Manifesto of Woman to the Foreign Office, and to the London embassies of the potential belligerents. Among those who signed the manifesto for IWSA were England's **Millicent Garrett Fawcett** and Scotland's **Chrystal Macmillan**.

> *We, the women of the world, view with apprehension and dismay the present situation in Europe, which threatens to involve one continent, if not the whole world, in the disasters and horrors of war. In this terrible hour, when the fate of Europe depends on decisions which women have no power to shape we, realizing our responsibilities as the mothers of the race, cannot stand passive by. Powerless though we are politically, we call upon the Governments and powers of our several countries to avert the threatened unparalleled disaster.*
>
> *Whatever its result, the conflict will leave mankind the poorer, will set back civilization, and will be a powerful check to the gradual amelioration in the condition of the masses of the people, on which so much of the real welfare of nations depend. We women of twenty-six countries, having bonded ourselves together in the International Woman Suffrage Alliance with the object of obtaining the political means of sharing with men the power which shapes the fate of nations, appeal to you to leave untried no method of conciliation or arbitration for arranging international differences to avert deluging half the civilized world in blood.*

On 1 August, Germany declared war on Russia. On the 2nd, the Germans demanded free passage through Belgium, whose rulers refused to grant it. On 3 August, Germany declared war on France. On Tuesday 4 August, Germany invaded Belgium. That evening at London's Kingsway Hall a women's anti-war rally took in a platform

The International Board of Officers from the International Woman Suffrage Alliance (IWSA) visit the House of Commons in July 1914

1914 Voluntary Aid Detachments (VADs) were established in 1909 to provide medical assistance in wartime. By summer 1914 there are over 2,500 detachments in Britain manned by 74,000 VADs, two-thirds of them women. (Dame) Katharine Furse takes the first VAD unit to France soon after the outbreak of war, establishing a hospital at Boulogne. Between 1914-18, 38,000 VADs work as assistant nurses, ambulance drivers and cooks; VAD hospitals are also opened in most large towns in Britain

1914

Millicent Garrett Fawcett, member of the IWSA and President of the National Union of Women's Suffrage Societies (1897-1919).

not think that Britain couldn't walk in and wipe them up.

In Russia the declaration of war alarmed **Florence Farmborough**.

We heard it at the country house. I remember how the news was so dreadful for us that we looked at each other and could scarcely speak. I was thankful beyond measure to learn that England, France and Belgium had joined Russia like allies and they were prepared to accept the war gauntlet thrown to them by Germany. Then I knew that all would be well. We were quite intent on doing something to help Russia. The work that women could do in those days was very simple and very limited. But there was one enormous work that women could always do – hospital work.

Seventeen-year-old **Mary Lees** was a doctor's daughter from Wellington in Somerset, just out of school.

We had a funny old cook – had an enormous bosom, and an apron. And she rushed into the dining room – she didn't knock on the door. And my mother was writing letters.

'Oh, ma'am,' she said, 'oh ma'am, war! War!'

I'd been out shopping and I came in and mother was cluttered in the dining room with two of her chums. I heard her say, 'Oh,' she said, 'there's a war. Yes, won't last very long, but Mary'll do everything for us. She's just left school. It's all right. She'll do the shopping and the cooking.'

So I thought, 'blow me, you will not. Mary's not going to do the cooking and the shopping.' So I went straight to the post office and I took out my savings. I had a very, very wonderful godfather. And I went straight out to see him. And I said, 'Look here, you've got to do something for me.' I said, 'I want to go on the first lot of people going on the land.'

Elizabeth Lee had been working in her father's toyshop.

I was on holiday. I don't think I had bothered much

from almost the entire pre-war women's movement, with the exception of Mrs Pankhurst's Women's Suffrage and Political Union. Its resolutions were sent on to 10 Downing Street.

Later that night Great Britain declared war on Germany. **Ruby Ord**:

Life was so normal and ran on an even keel, and this was something that threw everybody out of gear. Our friends – boyfriends – were rushing to join up. It was changing our lives completely. We all saw ourselves as Florence Nightingales. We had a sense of humour about it; we were funny, we had lots of laughs over it, because we didn't think it was serious, really. We did

1914

13 AUGUST First bombing raid of the war: a German aircraft drops hand grenades on Paris

14 AUGUST French aircraft bomb the Zeppelin sheds at Metz

22 AUGUST The British Expeditionary Force (BEF) meets German Army at Mons. Two days later the heavily outnumbered British withdraw, fighting an extended holding action known as the Retreat from Mons

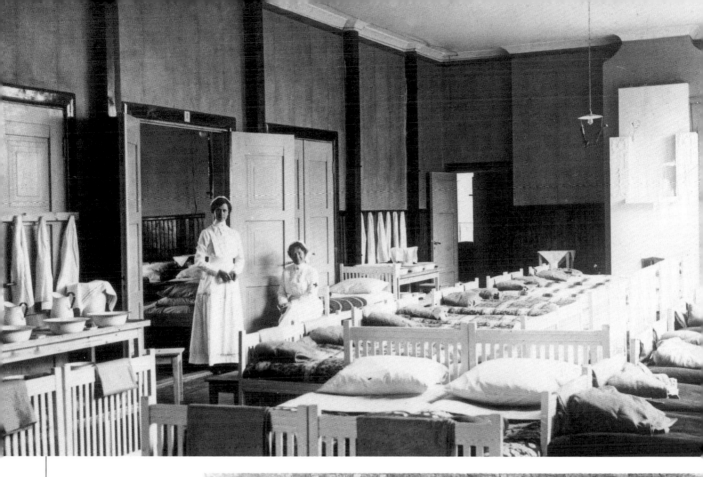

Nurses stationed at a hospital in Russia in 1915.

Female mechanics at work on a car at a Women's Volunteer Reserve motor garage in 1916.

26 AUGUST One of the BEF's two corps fights the Battle of Le Cateau, delaying the German advance by 24 hours and saving the Allied line

3-9 SEPTEMBER Battle of the Marne: the Germans are beaten back by a great French attack with the BEF in support; they retire to the line of the River Aisne and begin to dig trenches. The battle saves Paris from German occupation

1914

about it. You don't when you're young and having a good time. My brother and I could dance till three in the morning and get up and go to work. It didn't bother me in the least. I was one of those very fortunate people, and then I had umpteen boy friends in that time too. I could always get somebody to take me out. I wasn't a bit interested in the war.

Where I was staying we'd been fishing all the afternoon along by the riverside, and it was so peaceful and quiet, and I'd been saying how it was peaceful and we were going to go home and we were going to fry some chips. I was staying with a girl friend; I knew the family, we'd been to school together, and they'd moved away down towards Littlehampton.

So they said to me, 'You had better get home. We'll put you on the train in the morning; back you go home to your mum and dad, you can't stop here, we don't know what will happen.'

For **Alice Remington** her moment had arrived.

This was my big chance of getting out and away. I wasn't attracted to nursing and so I thought the next

Hard at work in the fields, a member of the Women's Land Army plays an important role in the home front war effort. (IWM: Q 30656)

13-28 SEPTEMBER First Battle of the Aisne: French and British forces attack again. As the opposing forces dig in, the lines of trenches extend as each side tries to outflank the other; ultimately, the trench system stretches from the Swiss frontier to the Belgian coast

19 OCTOBER-21 NOVEMBER First Battle of Ypres: the BEF suffers 13,000 casualties as it beats off repeated German attacks. The average strength of a BEF battalion, nearly 1,000 strong on landing in France in August, is now 1 officer and 30 men surviving unhurt

Young men queue outside the Whitehall Recruiting Office in August 1914, waiting to enlist. (IWM: Q 42033)

best thing I could do was to learn how to drive and how to do simple mechanics. My parents were a little bit horrified that I would meet the rough and rude men in the garage – quite true I did – but I didn't tell them very much really. I went out at about half past seven in the morning and I got home round about six at night, very grubby, and they just said, was I tired? Or something like that. They knew I would go off and do whatever I wanted.

Another teenager, in a world before teenagers, **Caroline Rennles**, from Camberwell, was working in a south London underwear shop.

We thought it was marvellous. My husband, he was only seventeen. Because he was a bit older than me, well I was courting him when I was twelve, you see, and when war broke out I was – fourteen? fifteen? – he went straight and joined up, with a lot of kids. They didn't realize what war was, no one did. Even the Boer War, love, we had nothing of it over here, did we?

20 OCTOBER British losses in the fighting to date: 57,000 men killed, wounded, missing, captured, or sick

24 OCTOBER Importation of sugar prohibited in UK

29 OCTOBER Turkey enters the war on the German side

9 NOVEMBER German light cruiser *Emden* sunk by the Australian cruiser HMAS *Sydney*

1914

CHAPTER TWO

GO HOME AND SIT STILL

IN AUGUST 1914 THE SCOTS DOCTOR, ELSIE INGLIS asked the War Office what she could do. 'My good lady,' she was told, 'go home and sit still.' She did not. Neither did large numbers of other women. Those women who opposed the war, at that time a predominantly middle-class minority, were faced with the realization that their brothers, sons and fathers might themselves be heading for the Front. One such was pacifist **Helen Pease**, whose father was to serve in France with the Royal Naval Division. She attended, with dismay, meetings addressed by Mrs Emmeline Pankhurst.

> *Mrs Pankhurst, heavens, she was patriotic enough. She was just like all the worst Tory women when it came to the war.*

Having completed her driving lessons **Alice Remington** resolved to get to France.

> *My father was secretly rather proud. He had no sons to send, the boy was only a nipper. Mother was horrified. She thought that – well, like all Victorian ladies she had never mentioned the facts of life to any of us and because of that she thought we should get into all sorts of trouble. We just as soon learnt.*

She became a Red Cross Voluntary Aid Detachment (VAD) driver, but her fellow drivers came from a familiar milieu.

> *The VAD drivers were drawn from the same social class. The mechanics at the garage weren't. The – how does one put it, the working class or what? – they went into the Women's Auxiliary Army Corps chiefly. I think because they hadn't the money to learn how to drive and at that time their class didn't have cars and do things in cars. Therefore to get into the war and do their bit it was much easier to go along with the stream and go to the WAACs.*

GO !

IT'S YOUR DUTY LAD

JOIN TO-DAY

Mother of war: a British recruitment poster. (IWM: PST 6540)

New roles and faraway places: the lure of the Voluntary Aid Detachment. (IWM: PST 3268)

Women coke heavers lift the fuel at a London gasworks.
(IWM: Q 30859)

Members of the Women's Auxiliary Army Corps utilize their skills as car drivers.
(IWM: Q 5746)

Elizabeth Lee's brother ran a garage, so she had learned to drive. After driving for the Red Cross in London she volunteered for the Army Service Corps and went on a month's trial.

We were each given one of these about thirty-hundredweight vans, and the men led us a devil of a life. They'd cut a petrol pipe half-through, they'd unscrew a valve on there, they'd change over the leads on the sparking plugs. They'd empty oil out of your lamps (because they was all paraffin lamps). The girls dropped out one by one. All this driving we used to do – they would give us the wrong directions. Some of us knew our way around the area but many of us didn't. And the sergeant backed the men up – he always gave us the dirtiest jobs to do, if it was a coal-heaving job we had to do it, or if it was to find an out-of-the-way place, it fell on the girls.

The men resented women in the army. Every time a woman went in the army, they were transferred elsewhere, out to France, you see, overseas, everything of that sort. At the end of the month there was just

17 NOVEMBER David Lloyd George, Chancellor of the Exchequer, introduces his first War Budget: £350,000,000 War Loan issued at 3.5%, redeemable after 10-14 years; Income Tax and Super Tax raised; prices of beer and tea raised

8 DECEMBER Battle of the Falkland Isles: von Spee's force is overwhelmed by British battle cruisers and cruisers under Sturdee. Von Spee, his flagship, *Scharnhorst*, and her entire crew are lost; only one German light cruiser escapes

two of us left. But they couldn't get much wrong with me, because I knew more than a good many of them did. And also I was cunning enough to always be prepared with a bit of stiff binding tape in case there was a leak in my petrol, and I looked at my tyres and tested them. When we had a tool inspection they'd pinch our tools, so that we were short of tools. You know, all sorts of nasty little niggly things that they'd do because they didn't want us. They wanted to try us out, because on the whole they were nice chaps; there were a couple of beastly ones, but to them it was a lark, for kicks.

Anyway, when we passed our test there were two of us that were taken on, they couldn't have been nicer to us; we were one of them then. And one of them said to me one day, 'Sorry we led you such a dance, but we didn't want women drivers, and we got our heads together and we thought we'd get a bit of fun out of these girls.' They wanted fun in other ways but it didn't work out. It did with some of them, but not with me.

Ruby Ord was to enrol with the WAAC when it was formed later in the war.

We were training two weeks. It was awful. We were at Hastings, which was very nice, but we had to get up about six and do PT and go for a march. We were drilled in the square, and were the laughing stock of all the men, which was absurd, because none of us had ever done this sort of drill that the army does – form fours and all sorts of section drill. So some people's right was my left and vice-versa. We then went for a route march before breakfast, and our last meal had probably been

1915 The restrictions against VADs serving at the front are lifted, allowing women volunteers over the age of 23 with more than three months' experience to serve on the Western Front, in Mesopotamia and at Gallipoli. Later, VADs are sent to the Eastern Front

1915 Women start to be employed for the first time in significant numbers as munitions workers, and for a wide range of other jobs; this includes recruitment into the armed services as auxiliaries, with the formation of the three women's services

1915

before seven the night before, and not adequate anyway – not for people straight from home, where mother took jolly good care that you had plenty, and a glass of milk before you went to bed.

We came back to terrible breakfasts: semi-raw herring and that sort of thing. You just couldn't eat it. So the little bit of money we had we spent as soon as we could get free from the fetters, and dashed to the nearest café.

We were also inoculated twice, and vaccinated – inoculated and vaccinated in one morning, so that quite a lot of the girls went down like ninepins. We were pretty miserable. And washing in tin basins in a room with a row of basins – well, we weren't accustomed to washing in company. So we were

WAAC members engage in the military-style practice of quick-marching.

adjusting very slowly. We had some very nice NCOs there, the Women's Voluntary Reserve. They were the suffragettes. But they had no control. Making troops of us I always resented. I didn't join an army, I always want to be a woman. I don't want to do anything that is imitating the men. I want the status of women to be established as women: I don't want to be given equality with men because I feel we are a bit superior. So that has always shocked me. I thought men used to look up to women. You don't look up to your equal.

1915

19 JANUARY First Zeppelin raid against Britain, hitting Yarmouth and King's Lynn

24 JANUARY Battle of Dogger Bank: British battle cruisers under Beatty sink the German armoured cruiser *Blücher* and damage other ships, including battle cruisers. Losses: British – 15 men killed, no ships; German – 1,000 men killed, 1 armoured cruiser sunk

OFF TO THE FRONT

Mairi Chisholm of Chisholm was eighteen, a Scot, and an aristocrat.

My brother was extremely fond of motorbiking and I was deeply envious; and my father who for that era was very open-minded gave me a motorbike. My mother was deeply opposed, but my father said, 'But why not? She's keen on mechanics and it's very good for her,' and so I had it. When war broke out I was very anxious to do what I could and I had the offer to go up to London and join the Women's Emergency Corps. My father said, 'Well, you've got your head screwed on all right and I'm not opposed to it; I think it's very natural for a young person to wish to do what they can in the circumstances.'

Many women volunteered their driving skills in various different units, including despatch riders for the Women's Emergency Corps like Mairi Chisholm, and British Army National Motor Volunteers, pictured in 1916.

22 APRIL–24 MAY Second Battle of Ypres: Germans launch a second major offensive, using poison gas for the first time, which helps to breach the British line. Canadian troops hold on, despite having no gas masks, and repeated German assaults are driven off

25 APRIL British and Empire – notably Anzac and French forces land at Gallipoli, in an attempt to establish a second front and knock Turkey out of the war. Operations quickly descend into stalemate in the face of fierce Turkish opposition, and both sides dig in

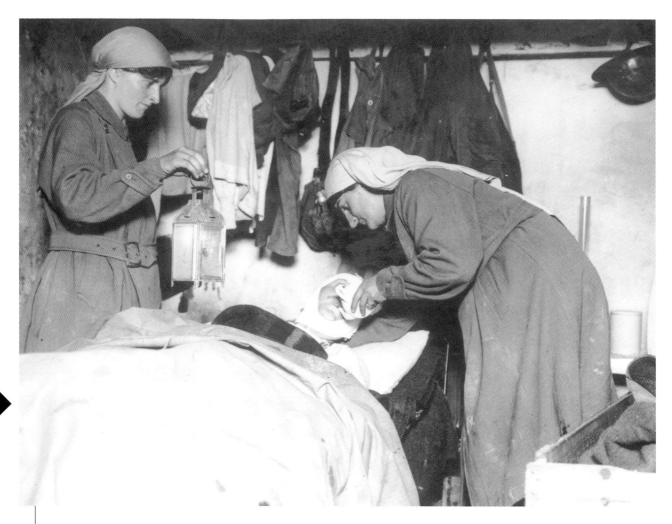

Mairi Chisholm and her colleague Elsie Knocker (later Baroness de T'Serclaes) tend a wounded Belgian soldier in a cellar dressing station in August 1917. (IWM: Q 2676)

My mother was terribly opposed and they started a very fierce argument. I went upstairs and collected some underclothes and things in a big handkerchief.

My mother said, 'I will on no account give her anything to take things away with her.'

I rode up to London on my bike, and went to the Women's Emergency Corps, which was situated in the Little Theatre in the Strand, and asked if

they'd like to have a despatch rider, and there I started. The Women's Emergency Corps was a remarkable thing; it was entirely manned by women, as you might say, by suffragettes, who had at once called off all their campaign and put themselves at the disposition of the government.

Dr Hector Munro who was then organizing the Flying Ambulance Column to Belgium was very deeply impressed with my ability to ride through the traffic. He traced me to the Women's Emergency Corps and said, 'Would you like to go to Flanders?'

I said, 'Yes, I'd love to.'

He was a great feminist in a time when that wasn't popular amongst men. He felt that women

29 APRIL Lloyd George announces the government's scheme regulating alcoholic drinks, aimed at ending drunkenness and absenteeism among munitions workers

7 MAY *Lusitania*, out of New York, torpedoed by *U-20* off the south-west coast of Ireland; 1,198 men, women and children perish; 124 of the dead are citizens of the neutral United States

should have more say in things, and he wanted to prove that he could take four women on to the battlefield and they would not fail. So he selected four, of which one was an American, Helen Gleason, and Lady Dorothie Fielding, one of the daughters of the Earl of Denbigh, myself and Mrs Elsie Knocker.

He volunteered direct to the Belgians, and they accepted him. We went out to all the battlefields immediately around Ghent. Mrs Knocker and I were walking along the road one day and we saw a sentry lying in the ditch and we thought, well, that's very curious, we must be walking past the last of the Belgian lines; and so we said to each other, 'Well, what does one do now?' Because obviously we'd gone a bit beyond where we should have gone.

So I remember saying, 'Well, let's go on, and then turn round at that corner,' and as we went still towards what must have been the German lines a car came along with three German officers fully plumed in their helmets and it drove straight towards the Belgian lines. They looked at us very closely and went on. The next thing we heard was machine-gun fire and rifle fire opened up, and we turned round and went back and these wretched Germans had really copped it, but one of them was only wounded. He said, 'Well, we saw two women walking, and we thought, well, we can't be into the Belgian lines yet.' And they got the lot.

In 1914 we were twice involved in bayonet charges. We heard the clash of steel and we hid behind a ruined wall until it was over and then had to clear up the situation, which was quite the nastiest because the Germans had, right at the sheath end of the bayonet, by the hilt, a saw, which was put there so that in the trenches they could cut up bits of wood and that sort of thing. I can't tell you what it was like when they put it through somebody's innards. The result of a bayonet charge was very disagreeable, very very nasty.

A Red Cross nurse meets wounded Belgian soldiers at a railway station.

12 MAY Anti-German riots in Britain

14 MAY An article in *The Times* highlights the shortage of munitions for the British forces; internment of 'enemy aliens' in Britain commences

18 MAY Speaking in the House of Lords, the Minister for War, Field Marshal Lord Kitchener, emphasizes the need for an adequate supply of munitions

1915

CHAPTER THREE

THE FRONT

GETTING THERE

EMILY RUMBOLD, A BAKER'S DAUGHTER LIVING in Bath, resolved that she would get to France. Later in the war, when the Women's Army Auxiliary Corps was formed, she joined it.

It was a beautiful sunset when we left Folkestone. It was too dangerous to go from Dover to Calais, so we went from Folkestone to Boulogne, and then halfway across, the moon came up – beautiful full moon, beautifully calm the Channel. We got almost to the quayside and we were ordered to take off our lifejackets and dump them down below, and as

Red Cross nurses help a wounded soldier in Flanders, 1914.

A WAAC recruiting officer enrols women applying to join the Women's Army Auxiliary Corps in Trafalgar Square. (IWM: Q 31082)

we drew up to the quayside the siren went for an air raid. So the boat promptly put out to sea again for an hour and it amused me intensely because we had no lifejackets on then. But then the raid was over and so we landed. My first reaction was 'I'm in France, I'm in the war!' I was excited the whole way through – it kept me going, I was in the war, and that's all I wanted to be.

There was the tramp, tramp, tramp, tramp of men going to the leave camp outside Boulogne, up on the hill. Another girl, who slept next to me – I never saw her before and I've never seen her since – we wanted to go out early in the morning, we thought it was so beautiful. We went out and oh! it was a picture. There was an old French woman with big baskets piled with apricots, golden apricots. It was a lovely September morning and the dome of the Notre Dame there up on the hill was peeping through the mist. It was a lovely start. You wouldn't have thought there was a war on.

Uniformed WAACs based in Etaples, France. (IWM: Q 8666)

BEING THERE

In 1914, in the wake of the retreat of the British Expeditionary Force from Mons, **Eleanora Pemberton**, in the Paddington 146 Red Cross Voluntary Aid Detachment, arrived in Boulogne.

One's impression was a good deal of chaos. There was a shortage of doctors, shortage of nurses, shortage of anaesthetics, shortage of everything. There were quite a number of nurses in the Queen Alexandra's Army Nursing Service – the QAs as they were called – stationed all over the world and they couldn't be got back in two minutes. A lot of them did come back. A great many more nurses were recruited for the reserve from civilian nurses in England; they wore a grey uniform with a red

23/24 MAY Italy joins the war on the Allied side

25 MAY Formation of Coalition government; Asquith remains Prime Minister; Lloyd George to become Minister of Munitions

23 JUNE Lloyd George introduces Munitions Bill

29 JUNE National Registration Bill introduced, providing for the registration of all people aged 15-65 in England, Wales and Scotland

A line-up of female ambulance drivers working in Etaples, France. (IWM: Q 2441)

border, the others wore the red capes, the reserves wore the red border.

Originally QAs were very snooty. They would have nothing to do with the VADs and weren't very keen on the reserve nurses either. The QAs were very select indeed. Some of them afterwards were very kind to us and nice, but later on when a lot of VADs were recruited to work in hospitals some of the QAs were horrible to them.

Ruby Ord:

We were lucky when we first went out. We had Mrs Kilroy Kenyon, the famous suffragette, as our AC. She also was a poetess. She was one who had been chained to Hyde Park railings and so of course to us she was a very famous person. She was very very good and she supported us. She fought for the girls

against the men because the base commandant, I think, resented our going there, and lots of the male officers resented our going out there; it was going to cause all sorts of complications, we would not be any good at the job, and 'Whoever heard of women doing this?'

Emily Rumbold was detailed to work in Calais docks, packing cleaned clothes taken from the dead and wounded.

They were being sent up the Line again and we had to pack them into sacks. As one sack was filled so you passed it on to somebody else. The WAAC officers were only in camp and they had jurisdiction of us out of working hours. The men officers were in charge of us all during the working hours.

If you wanted to move a heavy sack no man would help you. I remember once saying something or other that I wanted done and the man said, 'Oh well, you came over here to do any job, you jolly well do it.' He stood and watched me. They were very bitter at

8 JULY In a speech, Kitchener appeals for more recruits; Walter Long makes a statement on conscription, saying that while the National Registration Bill does not anticipate its introduction, the government has not discounted it either.

On the same day, the following message, typical of many at that time, appears in the Personal column of The Times: 'Jack F.G. If you are not in khaki by the 20th I shall cut you dead. Ethel M.'

1915

28 JULY Final debate in Parliament on compulsory military service; Asquith reviews the situation

4 AUGUST British losses for the whole year announced: 76,000 killed or died of wounds, 252,000 wounded, 55,000 missing – total: 383,000

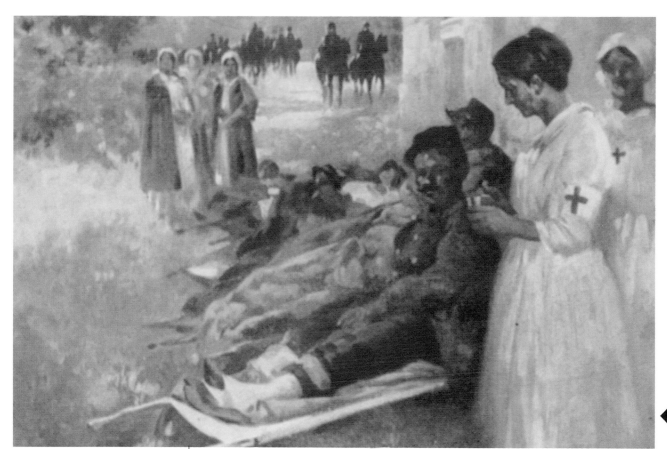

In a painting by Gilbert Rogers, a Red Cross VAD ambulance driver stands by the cab of her vehicle. (IWM: ART 3824)

Painting a pure vision: Red Cross nurses attend to wounded soldiers in France.

MUD AND SKIRTS

Ruby Ord:

The day before we sailed for France we were issued with uniforms, I think mine was down to my ankles. They were one-piece dresses with no shaping. We had to go to France, of all places, in this type of uniform. We were not allowed to wear gloves because we might look like officers. We had these terrible greatcoats that weighed a ton. The uniform was a disgrace to anybody – an orphan is better turned out than we were.

When we arrived in France, it seemed to rain all the time. The roads were liquid mud, and trailing skirts in the mud – we asked if we could be allowed to turn up the dresses, and were told they must be nine inches from the ground. A big notice was put up in the camp, and we changed that to nine inches

first but they got used to us.

I was still thrilled at being there, I was thrilled at doing the job that I was doing. But we missed colour – it was all khaki and mud; that was my chief memory. We thought we'd try and get a room, where we could buy our own cushions and have a little bit of colour there, and do as we liked. We found that it wasn't at all feasible because all the better-class people in Calais had all left. It was only the almost undesirables that had been left. We went to the doors and – 'There are officers already here.' We fled.

from the waist: we didn't know about mini-skirts. We decided amongst ourselves, the rebels – after all, we were suffragettes, a number of us – and we said, 'We are going to cut them off at the length we want so that they can't make us let the hems down.' So we just cut them off at the length we wanted and bound them round. It was quite a respectable length but not to their way of thinking. As you walked the mud splashed up, and we had only one dress. So if it was filthy dirty, you had to wear a filthy dirty dress.

As a VAD ambulance driver **Alice Remington** was not overly impressed by her uniform, either.

Navy blue, quite straight and quite ugly, a pocket here and a pocket there and the hats haven't changed very much until recently. They had a round piece turned up in front, and then we drivers had a peak cap later on. We were very proud of that – it was our distinguishing mark. The uniform was so loosely fitting that you could wear lots of woollies and things underneath. We had rather a mixed collection of clothes, which we wore on top when nobody was looking. I remember a Canadian officer gave me a most magnificent leather flying coat all lined with fur and I put this on with great joy and was considerably ticked off – but I was warm.

Emily Rumbold:

We didn't alter our skirts straight away. Our camp – we had duckboards, and outside the camp, you had to splosh through mud and water. We had them cut off then. They weren't short like mini-skirts, and I don't suppose they were more than halfway up your leg but they were shorter. We were the pioneers of short skirts. Some of the girls would put a bunch of flowers in their waist belts, or turn the collar of their frocks in the summer time. If they were found out, they got punished for it. I think uniform's uniform. It looked so horrible to have one wearing a bunch of flowers and one wearing a different collar, a silk collar. And then if you were on parade it would look so awful.

Dressed in fur coats, a group of First Aid Nursing Yeomanry (FANY) drivers, stationed in the French port of Calais. (IWM: Q 4669)

25 SEPTEMBER–15 OCTOBER Battle of Loos: combined British and French assault aimed at relieving the pressure on Ypres to the north. Casualties: 50,000 British, 140,000 German, 190,000 French. The British use gas for the first time, but despite considerable initial success, German counter-attacks restore the line

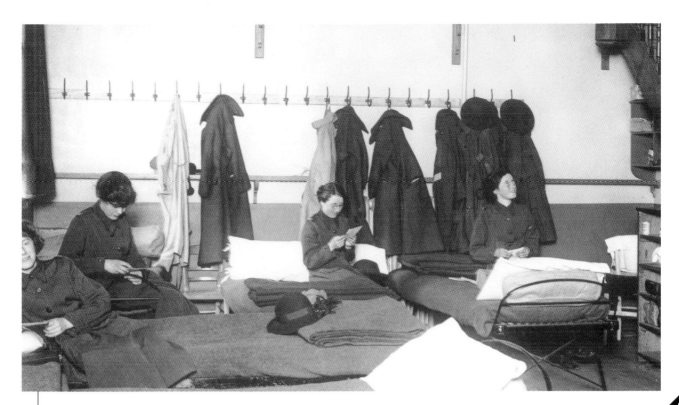

WAACs occupy a dormitory in Rouen. (IWM: Q 5757)

Ruby Ord:

We had those dark brown collars. So we bought light ones, which we weren't allowed to wear, but which we continued to wear. This is one of the things one learns early in life – if enough of you do something there is nothing that can be done about it. So it was a question of esprit de corps, our corps, not theirs! Enough of us wore these lighter collars so that eventually they ignored them.

Emily Rumbold:

We were the pioneers of short hair. A Frenchman cut my hair and did it beautifully – I've never had it cut so nicely since. He'd partly served his time in London. It was all bobbed hair; it was most attractive. They used to call me Mop after that. Some of the girls – their heads were not clean, that's why I had mine cut short. My mother was horrified

when I arrived home and found I had short hair.

We had nowhere to wash our clothes. You were not allowed to hang a thing up, not even a pair of stockings, in the hut. My pay was twenty shillings on paper, fourteen shillings was taken away for keep – your rations – and, included in the fourteen shillings, eighteen pence of that went for laundry. It was no good sending to the army laundry so we sent our own laundry to French people, to little private cottages, and then we had to pay for it ourselves.

FOOD

Ruby Ord:

The rations were quite good but the food was badly handled, badly cooked, and nobody seemed to be worried. The officers had the same rations and their food was beautifully served. I used to go over to the farm and have an egg beaten up in milk. The milk was warm from the cow and the egg fresh from the

5 OCTOBER British and French forces land at Salonika, in neutral Greece, to aid the Serbians against the Bulgarians. Half a million Allied troops are in Salonika by the end of the campaign

12 OCTOBER Edith Cavell, an English nurse serving in a Red Cross hospital in Brussels, is executed by a German firing squad for aiding the escape of British soldiers from Belgium

1915

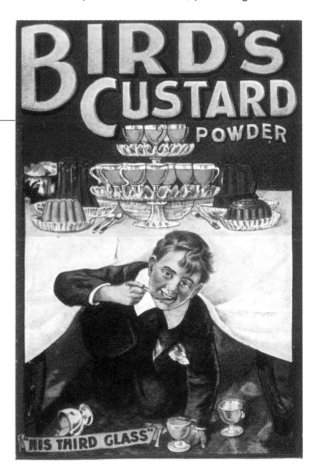

could help themselves. This was a very good idea; they are rich in iron and sugar sweet — good sugar, not refined sugar. That helped. Then there was the YWCA where we used to go and have malted milk, spending our own money, packets of biscuits, bars of chocolate. We used to dance in there too, in the winter, to warm ourselves up. There was no heating in the camp: it was terrible in the huts. There was nowhere to dry anything. It toughened us. I was certainly fit. I have never been so well.

Alice Remington had arrived in France working with Lady Angela Forbes's canteens.
There was plenty of tinned salmon right through that war. That was the favourite that the soldiers liked, good old wad and these French breads, and a mixture of melted-down butter, if not margarine

An American poster advertising the Young Women's Christian Association (YWCA). Together with its brother organization, the YMCA, it provided social services for the women and men in France.

An advert for Bird's Custard, served with prunes and figs by Alice Remington to the soldiers, and part of Britain's folk-memory.

chicken, and then I would buy fruit, which we were forbidden to buy, but I couldn't live without it. We had meat and some vegetables, but we never had green vegetables. We had a Canadian doctor — Dr Douglas, a woman — and when she came she objected to the army biscuits. She said they were causing anaemia, and she had raisins made available so that the girls

20 DECEMBER-9 JANUARY 1916 Allied forces evacuated from Gallipoli. Casualties: British, Dominion and Empire — 41,000 killed and missing, 78,500 wounded; French — 9,000 killed and missing, 13,000 wounded (plus another 100,000 Allied casualties through sickness); Turkish — 66,000 killed and missing, 152,000 wounded

In a watercolour by William Hatherell a Red Cross nurse sits by the bedside of a dying soldier, taking down a letter. (IWM: ART 5234)

which wasn't nearly as good as it is now, and salmon, mixed up in a whole big bowl, and you split it open and spread this great wad of salmon and butter, put them together. We sold hundreds of those.

The other thing was custard – how I remember the Bird's Custard Powder and two people with a big kettle pouring it in and swinging it round. And they had with that chiefly prunes and figs, but on high days and holidays we managed to get some peaches and tinned milk – that was the thing. And if it went round the camp that Angela – she was always called Angela – Angela's got peaches and cream, everybody

came tearing up. You could charge what you liked for it, which we didn't.

Ruby Ord:

We had plenty of outdoors – everything was al fresco, the fresh air was coming in everywhere. We used to paste up draughts with brown paper. We used to put brown paper between our blankets to increase the warmth. We found a way of looking after ourselves. We had rotas for baths – tin baths, and you were lucky if the water was hot on your night. But we were reasonably clean, and that didn't worry me too much, so long as we weren't lousy, and none of us were. We had plenty of Keatings [anti-louse powder] we used to sprinkle on our blankets.

1916 The Royal Navy becomes the first of the armed forces to recruit women. The Women's Royal Naval Service (WRNS) takes over the roles of cooks, clerks, wireless telegraphists, drivers, code experts and electricians. The women are so successful that other organizations such as the Women's Army Auxiliary Corps (WAAC) and the Women's Royal Air Force (WRAF) are established. When the Armistice is signed, the WRNS comprises 5,000 ratings and nearly 450 officers

1916

UNDER FIRE

Soon after the outbreak of the war **Antonia Gamwell** started driving for a French-controlled Red Cross unit.

It was well up in the Belgian lines – in a field. We were put in one corner and the Germans suddenly plugged the shells into this far corner of the field. We thought that was rather poor business.

Ruby Ord stayed in Calais to be bombed.

We had a woman called Stackhard – she was professional stage. She was a motor driver, a transport driver, and very, very good at her job. We were in this hotel and a raid started. All the staff of the hotel went down to the basement and they told us we could do so too, but we didn't. You were in the dark immediately in the old war when there was a raid – no blackout: everything was just switched off at the mains.

We had got two officers there, suffering from shell-shock and the men with them were in a panic. And Stackhard felt her way to the piano, and she played for two hours while the raid lasted, and we all sang and these men didn't know there was a raid on. Afterwards the men were so overwhelmed at her courage and her staying power, they said, 'If anybody ever says a bad word about the WAACs they'll have to answer to us for it after this.' Because people were very ready to criticize us, especially when we came home on leave; it was terrible. We were the women who had 'followed the men to France'.

There were several incidents like that, where the

WAACs stand to attention, lined up for inspection outside the Ministry of Labour, November 1917.

1916 As more men join the armed forces, the country grows short of labour. The government decides that more women must help to produce food and goods to support the war effort, and so the Women's Land Army is established. Many farmers resist the measure and in

1916 the Board of Trade begins sending agricultural organizing officers around the country, to persuade farmers to accept women workers. By 1917 more than 260,000 women are working as farm labourers or in the Women's Forestry Corps

girls showed outstanding courage. They really had it. In raids I didn't ever see anything that you could despise; and raids were new – we had had no previous experience of them. I really learned to admire women. I am a member of a family of women, because I have four sisters, and my mother I admired very much. So I was looking for their good traits, but I thought they were remarkable. They were so adaptable, so capable.

In all sorts of extraordinary circumstances they just set about it and did the job. A concert was needed. Some men had come out from the line and they were going over on leave, but they got a night in camp and they were getting drunk: could the WAACs put something on to distract them? You would probably arrive there and find that the concert platform instead of lights had got beer and stout bottles all the way round, and they were just going to shy at them. Then you would have a Scots girl go on and sing 'Loch Lomond' and they just melted. It was wonderful. I saw some marvellous things happen. I admired them tremendously.

CARNAGE

The main job of driver **Alice Remington** in Boulogne was picking up the wounded men from the trains.

The groans of people in pain are very distressing and there's not much you can do except get them there without making their wounds even worse. If you drove fast besides giving pain, which they might have stuck, you had to be so careful if there were

Wounded soldiers receive tea from a nurse by a railway carriage.

FEBRUARY In Britain, conscription is introduced for single men and childless widowers aged 18-41. The Military Service Act 1916 remains in force until April 1920, although conscription ends in 1919. The act provides for exemption on conscientious grounds, although it was left to those implementing the act to deal with each conscientious objector (CO) on a case-by-case basis. First limited signs of public opposition to the war among some sectors of British society – and notably among women – begin to appear

any fractures that the fractures didn't jag into anything, particularly if it was a chest wound. You couldn't have any ribs puncturing lungs.

They were astonished, the ones that weren't too badly wounded. 'Eh! It's girls!' – absolutely astonished. If they'd got what was known as a 'Blighty' they were absolutely on top of the world because they felt then, 'Well, at least I shall have a couple of months in the ward with clean sheets.' It was the dirt they hated so much, like me. The ones that had trench fever, and the ones that had dysentery, they were the most depressed. The ones that had a clean wound they were on top of their form. The ones who were very badly wounded lay there inanimate and just hoped that they weren't going to cry too much – that's what they were so afraid of. The very young ones that were very badly wounded, you could hear them, all the time, saying, 'Mother, mother'. If they'd been very badly wounded for three or four days their morale got so low. There is nothing more horrifying and depressing than continual pain.

If they were having what they called a push – absolute slaughter, I called it – and we had a lot of badly wounded people down, you might have five or six coffins a day to the cemetery. Then you could go for ten days without any. It depended entirely on how the war was going. The stretchers went flat up against the wall, you could put the coffins two on the floor and two above. All dreadfully primitive, horrifying, but you got used to it. If I wasn't to go back and do anything, I always tried to go and stand with the padre beside the grave because there were no other women there for these chaps, and I felt sometimes some of their mothers – might be sort of thinking of them.

When things were bad towards the end they couldn't supply enough wood and then it was just a question of blankets. That I didn't like because we had to go up to the mortuary, which was just an ordinary hut, and they had them 'named and numbered' and whoever had been dead longest, well, they had to be buried first. That was one job I did not like at all.

Mairi Chisholm:

There was one boy very badly hit in the head and the brain was emerging. And we had a discussion with the Belgian doctor from the trenches with us, as to whether it was worth trying to do anything about this fellow. The brain was damaged to the

Florence Farmborough sits outside her living quarters on the Russian Front.
(IWM: Q 107170)

Woman as saintly mother, depicted in a painting produced for a poster design.
(IWM: ART 5194)

21 FEBRUARY Siege of Verdun begins: the German assault initiates a series of attacks, counter-attacks and outflanking movements against a backcloth of massive artillery engagements

25 MAY Military Service Act becomes law, establishing compulsory military service for all men aged between 18 and 41, whether married or unmarried

31 MAY Battle of Jutland: British and German fleets meet at full strength. Losses: British – 14 craft, 6,097 men killed; German – 11 craft, 2,551 men killed. The battle's outcome undecided, the German fleet retires to port, never again to be an effective force in the war

5 JUNE Kitchener, Minister for War, is drowned when HMS *Hampshire*, carrying him on a mission to Russia, strikes a mine off the Orkneys

1916

Casualties of war: Russian soldiers lie dead on
a battlefield.

extent that it would never be right, and there were
masses of wounded coming in. We just opened up
everything and let the brain drop into a bucket.
That shows you what has to happen in certain
circumstances. The ones that were saveable – must
be saved.

Florence Farmborough became a field
nurse for the Russian Army, on its
southern front.

*During the very heavy engagements there was no
question of the soldier washing or changing his
clothes. They were fighting for life, day and night,
days on end. So many of them who came to us, the
first thing we did was to split up their trousers and
their waistcoats or suit, their uniform, and throw it
away. The very worst soldiers, the wounded soldiers,*

who came to us were the Turks. We had quite a few
when we were there on the Romanian Front. And
then it was not only throwing their blood-stained,
mud-stained clothing away – we literally had to
scrape their bodies of a most extraordinary crust
which seemed to have enveloped them during their
weeks and months on the Front. Sometimes they
were very upset about it. They preferred to have it
rather than be cleaned and have new pants and
shirts put on. But finally they succumbed and I'm
sure in the long run they were very grateful for
being clean once again.

A man who was dying asked, begged, for water.
And his eyes followed me everywhere. And he
prayed so earnestly and was so completely intent on
having something to drink that out of sheer
weakness and pity I gave him some. But it brought
about his death more quickly. But I never regret it
because after he had drunk he looked at me with a
tremendous look of gratitude in his eyes. I knew
that his passing would be eased. I did it more than
once and always I felt it was the humanitarian thing
to do when the case was hopeless. To the practised
eye it was easy to say within a few seconds whether
death would pass him by. I don't think you can
make a mistake; there is a stamp impressed on the
face, on the eyes, on the cheeks, on the whole colour
of the face.

In 1915 we retreated for five and a half
months. In 1916, when we advanced, the
battlefields that had once been so full of activity
and horror now were quiet; just littered with dead
bodies and completely smashed wire
entanglements. Even the trees themselves told
their story. Many of them, especially big forest
trees, were terribly mutilated and the trunks were
shaven down and the great tree branches were
thrown here and there due to the great and
dreadful cannonade that had swept over them. I
had thought before we had advanced, that now the
glory of our warfare would be seen in all its
wonder because I thought that can only mean

1916

1 JULY Start of the Battle of the Somme, a massive
British offensive, with French support, aimed at
relieving the pressure on Verdun. The British forces
suffer some 57,000 casualties on the first day, more
than 19,000 of them killed

13 NOVEMBER End of the Battle of the Somme.
Casualties: British – 420,000; French – 200,000;
German – 450,000. In contrast to the stalemate on
the ground, the Allied air forces have maintained air
supremacy throughout the battle

victory, victory and defeat of our enemies. But it wasn't. Walking over those battlefields was an experience so indescribably terrible, that it would never be possible to explain in ordinary words. One had to be there to see all that was left behind, the debris of the battlefield; men's crumpled bodies, great pools of stained earth, bits of clothing on the wire entanglements, guns thrown here, mutilation there. And then one asks oneself: so this is victory?

A nurse and soldiers at a British Army medical post at the front celebrate Christmas Day in 1914.

Alice Remington:

We had one particular Christmas, which was a really beautiful starlit night. It was Christmas Eve and a very big convoy came in but they weren't badly wounded. They were all very cheerful at the idea of getting into a bed with clean sheets, and we started singing, I think it was 'Hark the Herald Angels'. They all sang and it was such a very quiet, still night and you could hear, going up and winding up and down this hill, these boys singing their hearts out. It was a lovely thing, the moon shining and the stars shining and these boys all singing carols. They were so thankful, they knew they'd get a bath and be clean. I shall always remember that night.

5 DECEMBER Lloyd George succeeds his fellow Liberal, Asquith, as Prime Minister, having collaborated with the Conservatives to overthrow a man whose prosecution of the war, they believed, lacked vigour

18 DECEMBER End of the Siege of Verdun, the longest battle of the war, and the bloodiest engagement in history. Casualties: French – 542,000; German – 434,000. Verdun holds – just – which probably saves France

CHAPTER FOUR

BLIGHTY

THE CITY . . .

IN 1915 TWENTY-ONE-YEAR-OLD SCHOLARSHIP GIRL **Isabel Brown**, a skilled labourer's daughter from South Shields, got her first teaching job at one of the poorest schools of North Shields.

I was having children coming to school barefooted in the northern winter. The boy I'm thinking about, about nine he was, very blond. I could not reach that child at all. I had sixty children in a class, which was the norm. If a teacher was absent you got another thirty poked in. So you had ninety sometimes. But this child intrigued me. So one day I said to him: 'What did you have for your breakfast?'

He said, 'I never have any breakfast.'

I couldn't teach the child because he was hungry and deprived. I was reading in the local press once a week — we didn't have daily newspapers then — of the terrific casualties of the early part of the war. I made up my mind that humanity had advanced far enough to be able to run the world better than having hungry children, and murdering the youth of the nations — not only our own, but naturally I thought mostly of our own. The difficulty with hungry children and the terrible, terrible catastrophe of the war, hit me very badly.

A revolution in the British countryside and a poster to promote it.

. . . THE PLOUGH

In 1914 **Annie Edwards** was in service, in Pulborough. With the war she joined the Red Cross. Then, in 1915 she saw a poster for the Land Army.

I had to have three references. So I went to Canon Baggley's wife and asked her if she would sign. And she said she couldn't say anything bad about me at all. She admired me in every way of my life excepting she objected to me dressing like a man and it's going to spoil me. Because in those days that's the first time a woman, a female, ever wore

trousers, breeches or anything. I had my skirts right
down. Mustn't show your ankle.

She said, 'What are you going to wear?'

'Oh,' I said, 'they said breeches' – because I'd
already been to Worthing for the outfit. Oh, she was
against that.

But the Canon said, 'You can't go on that
breeches will alter her, because she's a good girl' –
because I was in the choir.

So in the finish she said, 'As much as I dislike
doing it I will do it.' Well, she couldn't do nothing
else. So she signed it. And the doctor signed it.
And my lady, where I was cook, she signed it. They
hoped it wouldn't alter my life.

I joined up.

Well, they said, 'You have been accepted in the
Land Army and we have found you a farm to do
your six weeks' training. And it's down at
Chichester.'

My mum was against that. 'We've brought you
up so strict. And do you know that's a barrack
town – soldiers?' She didn't like that. I said I didn't
go with soldiers. I hadn't been with nobody.

Father said, 'Good,' because there was more
money. And I said I could send some money home.
It all helped because children kept coming. Times
was hard.

The first week I come down to my billet, down to
the farm here, old lady stood over there. And I was
the first land girl she saw and she looked up

NATIONAL SERVICE
WOMEN'S LAND ARMY

APPLY FOR ENROLMENT FORMS AT YOUR NEAREST POST OFFICE OR
EMPLOYMENT EXCHANGE

A land girl ploughs a
field in a painting by
Cecil Aldin.
(IWM: ART 2618)

The animals came in two
by two . . . Woman the
provider at war.

Land Army girls prepare to go to market. (IWM: Q 30654)

through her glasses. She said, 'Huh! Neither a man or a woman.' I never had a long skirt on. Sort of a red-khaki breeches, you know, not exactly khaki but a bit darker than khaki, bit on the dark red side. We didn't like it at first. It made us sore. It was rough. There was rough inside. There wasn't proper seams. The machine was up and showed outside all right. Now, the inside was raw. And of course you wore your underclothes. That helped a bit. But it did [hurt] in different places and under your knees, until you got used to it.

The first year then, I was out in the field, harvest time, and wet through with sweat, wet through, right through this and all. In those days our corsets were severe, all steel bones and they got nasty. And when I put the horses in the stable at twelve o'clock I went up in the hayloft and I took them off. And close to the farm there was an outside lavatory, where they was emptied about every third year or

something. I went and folded them and took them there. And from that day to this I never wore them.

Mary Lees spent her eighteenth birthday on a farming course. Mrs Herbert, a local Land Army director, spoke to her about a delicate posting.

'Now, old Mr Tapp,' she said, 'he was married to a Miss Ridd. And nine months ago she bit a piece of cotton that was used to bind up the cattle suffering from anthrax. And she died in half an hour. And since then he's never spoken to another woman. Now,' she said, 'you have got to break the ice. He's got no help there and he's only got you to rely on.'

'Well,' I said, 'you don't want me to do much, do you?'

'Oh,' she said, 'I'll lend you two of my hunters, it's

JANUARY The House of Commons begins discussing the possibility of granting women the vote in parliamentary elections. Asquith, Prime Minister during the militant suffrage campaign, had always been against women having the vote. During the debate, however, he confesses he had changed his mind, and now supports the claims of the NUWSS, WSPU and the WFL

quite all right, you can ride.'

I got on to one of these wonderful hunters; they really were beautiful beasts. And I rode right up on to the moor, came into the yard. And there was old Tapp standing there. Very upright. Coal-black hair. Bright pink cheeks. Riding crop under his arm and sort of breeches with a sort of bulge. And gaiters. And in his hand he was holding a sack and a pair of shears. He didn't take the slightest notice till I got off the horse. I came round the horse.

'Put her over there in the shed,' he said.

I took her over, put her in the shed. I came back. Still he didn't speak. I thought, well, what the hell's the matter with him?

He handed me the sack and the shears. 'Now,' he said, 'go up the road, first gate on the left down over; under the hedge,' he said, 'you'll find an old ewe. Her's been dead three weeks. I want the wool.'

So I thought, all right, try anything once, that's my motto. So I took them and I went down. I didn't need the shears. The body was bright blue. So I plucked off all the wool. And I sat her up in the hedge. I can see

her now with her feet sticking out like that. And I went back. And he was still standing there.

I said, 'Oh, Mr Tapp, I didn't need the shears because, you see, the wool really came out quite easily. I think perhaps I'd better have a spade, hadn't I, and bury her/it?' I didn't know what it was.

And do you know, he looked at me: 'Gor,' he said, 'you done it? I were testing you. Will you shake hands?'

Nine months after he wanted to marry me. Just like that.

PRODUCTION LINE

After the coming of the war **Jane Cox**, living in Mile End, began working at Schneiders, a factory making civilian and service caps. The

Over the top: members of the Women's Land Army smile for the war effort. (IWM: Q 30678)

JANUARY The government announces the establishment of a new voluntary service, the Women's Auxiliary Army Corps (WAAC). Although not given military status – members are enrolled rather than enlisted – women who join the corps

serve as clerks, telephonists, waitresses, cooks, drivers and as instructors in the use of gas masks. Between January 1917 and the Armistice over 57,000 women serve in the WAAC

1917

A member of the Land
Army milks a cow.
(IWM: Q 30680)

dye used for khaki clothing was toxic and
led to boils . . .

*If you stopped to blow your nose you got the
sack. You couldn't go to the toilet. You really
worked in those days. There was no
recompense for illness or anything else; no
holidays with pay. The one on my back was
worse. It was right on the spine. And we had
no treatment. It was just lucky that it really
cleared up because I never got any treatment
for anything at all. The women at work thought
my mother was terrible not to look after me.
But my father was dying.*

*Then when my young sister died, all my
mother was interested in was bringing home a
few shillings. I started to get clothes. And no
sooner I'd bought anything my mother'd pawn it.*

'Munitionettes' – producing the explosives and
gas that comprised the raw material of war –
were the largest group of women workers
engaged in war activity. A job in a munitions
factory could mean a vast increase in the pay
on offer before the war. Sixteen-year-old
Isabella Clarke, locked in poverty in Roman
Catholic Belfast, made the crossing to White
Lund in Morecambe, where she worked at
filling 9.2-inch gas shells.

*We weren't allowed to wear any of our clothes. If you
had linen buttons on – there was tin inside, you see,
and it would cause an explosion. We were also
supplied with cocoa going on duty and coming off
duty, and we had our own surgery and doctor. And we
were supplied with rubber shoes – pumps, really –
and they were all platforms from the entrance of the*

8 MARCH Revolution breaks out in Russia; a week
later Tsar Nicholas II abdicates

28 MARCH The Women's Auxiliary Army Corps
(WAAC) is formed

APRIL Called 'Bloody April' by the RFC. In
attempting to support the Allied offensives at and
around Arras, British pilots suffer heavy casualties,
amounting to one-third of the RFC's strength. First

factory to the department wherever we worked. Your feet never touched the ground, and there was soldiers on guard all the way round.

They could always tell by the colour of our eyes whether the gas was affecting us, and unfortunately we were coming home for our Easter holidays and my friend was stopped. They noticed that both her eyes and mine – the white of my eyes was discoloured a little bit, but hers was badly. Then they come and informed me that she'd died. Very little of this gas, once it got into your inside, did affect you. Your hair didn't go yellow but when you went to bed, as you took your head off the pillow, the pillowslip was pink. I was fortunate, my friend refused this herring that was cooked for us and I was a bit greedy and I ate mine and hers. It made me sick. Being bilious after the herring it was what really saved me.

My friend being dead, it upset me and when I went back to Morecambe there was an explosion and I decided to leave. I wanted to go to London to Woolwich Arsenal and they told me in the labour exchange no, that I was too young, but they were going to send me to Coventry. I said, 'Is Coventry near London?' They told me, 'Yes.' I was that ignorant, I thought it was only a tram ride, so I came. I used to send my mother a pound a week and my grandmother five shillings. The first time I went home she wanted to know how it was I had such nice clothes and such a lot of money.

Born in Blackfriars, the daughter of an electrical engineer **Annie Howell** took a job in a factory making gas masks.

The war never sunk into me, that the war meant they'd got to kill each other to win. It never entered my head. I just knew it was a gas mask. One day, I said to this girl, 'This gas mask, what's it for – where do they put the gas?'

'Oh, no,' she said, 'they don't put the gas in it. The Germans' – always the Germans, never us – 'the Germans throw gas bombs over and they gas the men.'

'Oh,' I said. I was a bit ignorant in lots of ways.

Lilian Miles lied about her age – she was thirteen when war was declared – to get a munitions job at White and Poppe's in Coventry.

I knew a girl that had been out the night before with me. And with the blackout someone gave us a couple of matches to light the candle when we got in our room. She used one match. Next morning she went to pull her handkerchief out when we were in the works. And out flew this match. The foremistress saw it. They suspended her right away. I tried to tell them it was quite accidental. And they said it didn't

The money earned by 'munitionettes' was another reason women headed for the factories. (IWM: PST 0402)

appearance of German 'flying circuses', units of 4 squadrons – up to 50 aircraft – operating as a whole. The German habit of painting their aircraft in bright colours earns these units their nickname

6 APRIL The United States of America declares war on the Central Powers (Germany, Austria-Hungary, Turkey and Bulgaria). US troops will not go into action in France until early 1918, however

1917

matter what I said. Proceedings would be taken. She was brought into court next day. They just said 'Twenty-eight days.' They took her away to prison, to Winson Green. And she never got over it. Within a few months she died. She was twenty years of age.

Munitionettes – 'Tommy's sisters' – were also known as 'canaries'. **Lilian Miles**:

The yellow powder turned us yellow all over. I had black hair and it was practically green. Once you come out of it it wore off. Within a couple of weeks it was gone. But while you were in it you were yellow. You'd wash and wash and it didn't make no difference. It didn't come off. Your whole body was yellow.

Caroline Rennles, born in Camberwell, was fifteen in 1914. She took a job filling shells in Slades Green.

These old conductors used to say in the train, 'You'll die in two years, cock.'

So we said, 'Well, we don't mind dying for our country.'

Elsie McIntyre, sixteen in 1914, was working at the Barnbow National Shell Factory in Leeds.

We were filling 4.5[-inch], 18-pounders and 6-inch

Women at work in a shell-filling factory, Chilwell, Nottinghamshire. (IWM: Q 30011)

9 APRIL-16 MAY Battle of Arras: Canadian troops take Vimy Ridge among other gains. Casualties: British – 150,000; German – 100,000

16 APRIL-15 JUNE The French launch a great offensive, known as the Second Battle of the Aisne or the 'Nivelle Offensive'. Gains are of the order of 600 yards, and the attackers suffer terrible casualties

shells. We had a fortnight in the powder and after the fortnight we had a fortnight on the stencil side. That was the dirty side. You could only do a fortnight. And then you had to come out, owing to the poison. And it was those people that you saw going about, they had yellow hands even through the gloves. We had two half-pints of milk a day to keep out the poison from the powder.

With war **Helen Pease's** father became an officer in the Royal Naval Division, while she became a pacifist. After attending the

Women's Trade Union College she briefly became active in the Women's Trade Union League.

At Hayes Munition Factory they'd got five thousand girls. Most of these girls'd never been in a factory before. They'd probably done home sewing, the sort of things they did, London girls, when they wanted to earn their livings. The management was all men.

One day the telephone came through to the office in Bloomsbury. 'For God's sake send some of your organizers down here. The girls are all hysterical. And they've chased me into the office.' The manager, if you please. 'I've locked myself in.'

Madeline Simons and I were off down there. We found five thousand girls, raging hysteria, shrieking, yelling and throwing the furniture about.

Young female munition workers operating lathes at a Midlands factory. (IWM: Q 108394)

7-14 JUNE Battle of Messines. The Germans have occupied the Messines Ridge since early in the war, thereby dominating the Ypres Salient. General Plumer's Second Army assaults the ridge following the explosion of 19 huge mines. The attack is a triumphant success; the British take and hold the ridge until the massive German assault during the Battle of the Lys, 2-29 April 1918. For the first time, British casualties in attack are fewer than the defending Germans'

The art of war: women working on the production of 15-inch shells in a Glasgow factory.
(IWM: ART 2271)

'For King and Country', by Edward F. Skinner. Female workers attend machinery in a munitions factory.
(IWM: ART 6513)

Madeline Simons stood up, a very beautiful woman with a Parisian dress on, and talked to them in a quiet way. And finally we got them to choose some of their number to make a committee to join the union to come and talk to the management.

The row had officially arisen, or the reason the girls gave – and this shows what happens when you

get a crowd of people in a state of exhaustion and tension and so on – well, somebody had found a cigarette end in the rice pudding. Madeline and I got these, a group of about eight girls, to go along and see the manager. He said to us. 'I'm quite used to dealing with men. I've never had to deal with women before. For heaven's sake go up and keep them

17 JULY By order of King George V, the royal family's surname is changed from Saxe-Coburg-Gotha to Windsor. Other notable families follow suit – the surname of Admiral Prince Louis of Battenberg changes to Mountbatten

31 JULY Third Battle of Ypres (Passchendaele) – Haig's attempt to breach the German line and roll it up from the north. Tenacious German defence, coupled with appalling weather and ground conditions, make this a costly advance

A woman works on aeroplane propellor blades at the Frederick Tibbenham factory in Ipswich.
(IWM: Q 106589)

quiet.' It was really very funny, especially when you think we were both of us twenty-two and twenty-one and had no experience.

They produced some sort of settlement they were able to discuss and the girls, some of them, joined the union. And, you know, there was then some organization which could talk to the management.

There were no shop stewards, of course, no unions at all. And the men's unions wouldn't touch the women at that time. They didn't want women's unions and women to take men's work.

At Coventry Ordnance **Isabella Clarke** decided to join.

SEPTEMBER German bombers switch to night bombing

31 OCTOBER 22 Gothas bomb London, Essex and Kent. Damage is light, and 5 aircraft are damaged or destroyed

1917

A woman welder employed at an aeroplane factory near Birmingham. (IWM: Q 28182)

There was a good many Irish girls there. The question was would I join a union? I did and they did. We used to pay the money in – at that time the union was at the back of a Maypole in Broadgate – the Transport Workers' Union, and it was where they put me right about the rates. That's how I got the rate.

GOOD LIFE

Working at Coventry Ordnance, and living in the hostel, **Isabella Clarke** made six times the money she had earned in Belfast.

The same seats was always reserved in the circle every week for the Hippodrome, and on a Monday, not having to start till five o'clock we used to go to the matinée at the Empire. There was every facility in the Coventry Ordnance hostel for you without going out at all. There was a nice hall and there was a piano in it and there was dancing and singing and parties. We had a bathroom, we had a room to ourselves and we had a maid. And the maid used to make our beds and we had the stand with the toilet basin and jug there. And it was always washed and refilled with water. And when you come in from work you could go straight away in the Ordnance and have a bath.

The world of **Jane Cox** also expanded.

London was a swinging place. People from the East End started going up the West End. There was quite a division between the rich people and the poor people. My sister and I used to go to shows. There was all sorts of different forces here all centred round the Strand and Trafalgar Square. You went round the square and they'd all be sitting round the fountains. And it was interesting. We used to count up how many boys we'd speak to, what different nationalities. In the Strand there was a hut where the forces could go for refreshment or entertainment. And in the Aldwych was another place. And some of the soldiers were so grateful if an English girl would speak to them and, oh, we used to get on very, very well. I was taken out to cinemas and treated. There was one place in the Strand, and the girls used to come round with boxes of grapes and boxes of chocolates. The boys used to be only too pleased to spend their money. I had a fabulous time even though I was engaged. I got married so quick because when my husband came home from sea, neighbours kindly told him how I . . . So on a three-day licence we got married.

There was always excitement of boys on leave. Life was beginning to be for living. Before that it was just working and sleeping and eating when you could

6 NOVEMBER Third Ypres ends as Canadian troops finally take the village of Passchendaele and the remaining objectives. Casualties: British – more than 300,000; German – under 200,000. Damage to the morale of British troops is considerable

6-7 NOVEMBER The 'October Revolution' in Russia (Russia still uses the Julian Calendar, which in 1917 is 13 days behind the Gregorian used in the West). Supported by revolutionary or disaffected elements of the navy and army, Lenin, in hiding since

get it to eat. But it was just the excitement of it, all the foreign forces here and the little bits of luxuries you got from them. It was really a marvellous time. We went up to town. We'd seen places we never even thought we'd see. There was a place near Tottenham Court Road, called Frascatti's, one of these very posh restaurants. And my boyfriend home on leave said to me he wanted to take me up in town. And I said, oh, I wouldn't go. I never thought of going up to town.

My mother said to me, 'Why don't you go, Jane? You'll be all right.'

I was only about sixteen. And I had a navy-blue coat. And I had a black velvet beret that I'd made

Women who moved to London to join the war effort, and Eastenders like Jane Cox, would go to the West End and gather at lively places such as Piccadilly Circus.

myself, because working in the caps, I knew how to do it.

And he took me to this Frascatti's. There was all officers sitting there with all the ladies done up to the nines. And my boyfriend took me right to the front. And a waiter came up and asked me what tune I'd like the band to play.

When we ordered, I didn't know what he was going to order, so we ordered scrambled eggs. So the waiter said, 'If you're not going to have a proper meal you have to sit at another table with just a drink.'

I don't know how I got out of that place. That was my first introduction to high society. There was all these ladies with hats with plumes on and furs, and the officers. It was gorgeous. And I tell you I was a very shy sort of person. My boyfriend said it was like taking out a wooden doll. I'd stutter and stammer and blush. I had no art of conversation, nothing at all. But they were the days.

July after an abortive Bolshevik attempt to seize power, leads a revolt against the provisional government. By the 8th the Bolsheviks are in power

8 NOVEMBER Lenin reads his Decree on Peace to the new Soviet Congress; by now, Russian armies fighting on the Eastern Front have collapsed

1917

JOURNEY'S END

The casualties from the shells and poison gas arrived from France at stations like Charing Cross, at night. They went into the care of nurses like **Margaret Warren**, by then a Red Cross VAD nurse, based at Brooklands Hospital, south of London.

> They were very often very shocked, probably extremely dirty if they'd just recently come from the trenches, very thankful to be out, but probably in great pain, and the antidotes for pain were very poor; there was aspirin, we had morphia – and morphia was not given except by an injection, one little tablet of morphia put into a teaspoonful of water, and you had to wait until this little tablet had dissolved, then you sucked it up into the needle, and tried to find a good place to give this injection.
>
> Many of the men had the most frightful carbuncles and terrible boils and things from the very bad conditions they'd been in, and as we had no penicillin then they had to be got out of their system in some way.
>
> When I found that a limb had to be removed, the soldier would say to me, 'Nurse, you will come into the theatre with me, won't you?' The first time I was there, there was a great big Sergeant Dunn – a very charming man – and he had to have his leg amputated, and I'd been trying so hard to get this leg better, and there I was left with this leg in my hand, and the doctor turned to me and said, 'Well, put it in the bucket, nurse.'

Caroline Edgley, a Red Cross VAD nurse in her twenties, was based at the 4th Northern General Hospital in Lincoln, where she received soldiers whose last treatment had been at a casualty clearing station in France.

15 DECEMBER Peace, on ruinous terms for the newborn Soviet Union, signed between Russia and Germany at Brest-Litovsk. With Russia out of the war, large numbers of German and Austro-Hungarian troops, as well as huge amounts of matériel, are released to fight the Allies on other fronts – notably the Western Front. Civil War breaks out in Russia, which continues until 1920

London's Trafalgar Square: in two world wars it was a place for brief encounters, dangerous liaisons, fleeting friendships, and lifelong partnerships.

Painting of an advanced dressing station in France, where many casualties were brought by stretcher-bearers. (IWM: ART 1922)

Wounded men arrive at Dover station by hospital train. (IWM: ART 1273)

1918 British bombing raids against Germany begin. By October 1917 day and night raids are being made by the RFC and RNAS, and by 1918 squadrons are bombing German cities, airfields, factories and military targets

1 JANUARY Rationing for individuals introduced in Britain, principally of sugar, tea, margarine, bacon, cheese and butter. National meat rationing is introduced in April 1918, and on 14 July coupon books for meat, fats, sugar and lard are issued

1918

A Voluntary Aid Detachment (VAD) nurse. (IWM: Q 31011)

A group of nurses based at a Red Cross hospital during the First World War.

They'd have just one dressing put on their bare wounds and put on a train again. And they landed at Lincoln Station and brought straight up to the hospital with all the clothes that they'd been wearing for the last six weeks or more. You'd have to peel it off them. One man after he'd been washed and dressed said he thought he must be in heaven. He eventually had to have his leg off. Taken into this big tent and they'd be sawing his leg off.

1918

21 MARCH-5 APRIL First phase of the 'Ludendorff Offensive': massive German attack also known as the Second Battle of the Somme; a last-ditch effort to win before the growing numbers of US troops in France are pitched into battle. British armies, pierced in several places, fall back, and French forces retire to conform. Exhaustion eventually halts the Germans after an advance of 40 miles. Their casualties, however, have been almost as great as the Allies'

Edith Evans, who was fifteen at the outbreak of war, became a VAD nurse with the 36th detachment of the Red Cross, and was sent to Kent.

It was a lovely billet with a private family in a beautiful home with a lovely garden where they used to call me their 'third daughter'. I was there eight months and that was the best of all. They were intensely musical and Mrs Matthews, the mother, arranged a concert every single Monday for four years in that hospital for the soldiers. And we used to have a little band; I played the violin and I used to sing so I took part in the concerts. They used to call up the stairs, 'Your turn next, Sister', and down I had to rush from my work and perform and go back again – and that really was very nice.

There was one other lovely musical event in the hospital; every Friday morning the Marine String Band came and played in the hall for the soldiers and that really was a highlight of the week – it was beautiful. Doctors always like to operate on a Friday because, they said, the men went under better with the music going on.

28 MARCH The House of Commons votes by 341 to 62 to enfranchise women over the age of thirty who are householders, the wives of householders, occupiers of property with an annual rent of £5 or more, or graduates of British universities. However, MPs reject the idea of granting the vote to women on the same terms as men

REVOLT AND REVOLUTION

CONCHIES

FOR WOMEN OPPOSED TO THE WAR IT HAD BEEN a long, dispiriting road. In April 1915 a women's peace congress had taken place in The Hague. One hundred and eighty British women wanted to attend. None did – the Royal Navy closed down the North Sea.

Three British women, already abroad, did attend, and were denounced in the *Daily Express* as 'pro-hun peacettes'. Out of the meeting came the Women's International League For Peace And Freedom. Emmeline Pankhurst and her daughter Christabel had parted company with the other Pankhurst daughter, Sylvia, a vigorous socialist

Mother and daughter women's suffrage campaigners, Emmeline (right) and Christabel Pankhurst.

Sylvia Pankhurst, daughter of Emmeline and younger sister of Christabel, who founded the East London Federation of Suffragettes.

opponent of the war, who had set up the East London Federation of Suffragettes. Sylvia braved imprisonment, force feeding, physical attacks. **Helen Pease** remained sceptical.

Sylvia irritated me profoundly. I didn't like her ways. I didn't think she was truthful, always rather hysterical, I thought, and, I fancied, a great deal too much thinking of her own position. I don't mean that she wanted to go up in the world. I mean she wanted to be regarded as the head agitator. And she was the agitator. And any other agitators who didn't agitate the same way as she agitated were simply not worth speaking to. I didn't like any of the Pankhursts much – Mrs was much the nicest. I didn't know them at all well but I met Sylvia. But she was so obviously totally uninterested in any work anybody else was doing, or any causes except the one she was espousing in which she was the prophet, that I'm afraid that I got rather fed up.

In 1916, at Verdun between February and June 1916, the French had suffered 315,000 casualties and the Germans 281,000. On 1

July 1916 the British Army endured the bloodiest day in its history. At the opening of the Battle of the Somme 40,000 soldiers were injured, missing or taken prisoner, and between 19,000 and 20,000 killed. The 'battle' dragged on until November. The British suffered 420,000 casualties, the Germans 450,000, the French 200,000.

At home the Defence of the Realm Act (DORA, forerunner of the Official Secrets Act) was used to harass, prosecute and imprison anti-war activists. In November 1914 the No Conscription Fellowship had been founded, but conscription, the enforced recruitment of men to the armed forces, did not follow until the beginning of 1916. It meant broader opposition to the war. Helen Pease was living in Cambridge:

My cousin Cecil was killed on the Somme in

Battle of the Somme, 1916: artillery bombardment occurs in the Somme Valley near Curlu.

September or October 1916. By this time most people were saying there ought to be conscription. And so the position of us pacifists became a little more difficult and we had to think out what would happen. There was no question then of conscripting women. But we had a meeting where the group formed themselves into the Cambridge group of the No Conscription Fellowship. I was made shadow secretary that time. A shadow secretary was there for when the real secretary was arrested.

In Britain, alone of the belligerents, conscription was accompanied by exemption for 'conscientious objectors', but treatment of 'conchies' could be brutal. And since 1914

The 'White Feather' flag is hoisted by women in London's East End, part of the pro-war wave which coerced men not in uniform.

men out of uniform had been the target of women handing out white feathers, as symbols of cowardice. Who gave out the feathers? **Elizabeth Lee**:

We would call them teenagers now but we were flappers in those days – fourteen-, sixteen-, seventeen-year-olds. You used to ride on the back of a motorbike and it was sidesaddle on the motorbike, you'd have an arm round the bloke's waist. Those were the people who'd chiefly do it. It was some

1 APRIL The RFC is amalgamated with the RNAS to create the Royal Air Force (RAF). Also formed is the Women's Royal Air Force (WRAF). Over the next 9 months the WRAF recruits 9,000 women, to work as clerks, fitters, drivers, cooks and storekeepers

12 APRIL The German attack on the Somme continues; Haig declares: 'With our backs to the wall, and believing in the justice of our cause, each one of us must fight on to the end.' The Allies continue to be driven back, sometimes in disarray

mothers whose sons were away, but I don't think it was so much them as the kids – they'd do it because their brother had gone or something like that, more often than not, or their dad had gone – their dad was fighting, and somebody else wasn't.

Ruby Ord, in France, loathed COs, as conscientious objectors were sometimes, confusingly, called.

I don't think I would have given a white feather, because I wouldn't know if a man had a sickness or something as a reason for not joining. But I still would despise people who were unwilling to fight. I used to go and speak at meetings.

Helen Pease observed the situation at Cambridge University.

When conscription came there was a good deal of – not legal, but attempted – molestation. Some retired colonel used to ask undergraduates to come and have tea with him and get their rooms searched while they were away. It didn't matter in the least and was quite illegal. We knew very well that in any other country there would be no question, they'd have been shot out of hand. So we knew very well that we were still lucky to be English, or most of us did.

Lilian Miles was working as a munitions worker from 1917 to 1918.

I used to think, well, if they object to war, good luck to them. It wasn't for me to say what they should do. I worked with a conscientious objector. Everybody else didn't speak to him. But I spoke to him. And I was friendly with him because I respected his views. I thought, well, if he objects to it, well, that's it. That's his business. He was only a young man. He was twenty-nine. I always remember him. I believe it was religious, on religion, that he objected.

Conscription meant court battles. **Helen Pease** followed the cases before tribunals at the old Shire Hall in Cambridge.

We always went to support them. It was an impossible position. The chairman of the bench was a very worthy market gardener, and to have a long argument between the officer of the Crown and a very vocal CO on what was the proper interpretation of the New Testament. I wrote to Father about it and said they were stupid old men. And they were, they were quite illogical, you see. And whereas they would give exemption or non-combatant service we never could discover on what principle they gave complete exemption to some and non-combatant service to others.

Crowds gather outside Parliament to watch delegates arrive at a Compulsion Debate to decide on the issue of conscription in January 1916.

27 MAY-2 JUNE Third Battle of the Aisne: Ludendorff's third great attack, launched against French positions on the Chemin des Dames, where the line is initially penetrated up to 13 miles. After further German advances, however, US troops hold the Marne crossings, capture Cantigny and go on to clear the enemy from Belleau Wood. The British line also holds, and by the end of the battle Ludendorff holds a 35-mile-deep salient aimed at Paris, but lacks the power to press his attack

1918

CHAPTER SIX

REDS AND YANKS

EARLY IN 1917 THE RUSSIAN EMPIRE COLLAPSED. The Tsar, Nicholas II, abdicated in favour of a provisional government. By then **Helen Pease** was working with the geneticist William Bateson in Cambridge.

It was the dawn of a new world. All of us radicals had been praying for a hundred years for the downfall of the Tsar. That March Father came sprinting down the passage of the flat shouting 'Revolution in Russia!' It was very cold-douching to find Bateson, who knew the Russians pretty well, and had a very poor opinion of the Russians: 'Never do any good, talk all night and never do anything,' which was fairly correct.

There was this meeting in the Albert Hall. They sang; of course they hadn't got a new national anthem – they sang the old Russian national anthem ['God Preserve the Tsar'], which was a very fine tune. And it wasn't only the liberals – everybody was there, because a lot of people felt something

Soldiers and workers gather on the streets of Petrograd during the Russian Revolution.

The last Russian emperor, Tsar Nicholas II, who abdicated in March 1917 after the Petrograd riots, following the resignation of his government and the first revolution of that year.

Vladimir Ilych Lenin,
leader of the Bolsheviks
responsible for
orchestrating the October
Revolution in 1917.
(IWM: Q 101743)

was at last happening. They believed the revolution people would fight like the French Revolution, would fight the Germans just as the French revolutionary armies had risen against them. It was a marvellous feeling. And this packed meeting at the Albert Hall! The singing of the national anthem and the speeches welcoming the new Russia, it was more like a revivalist meeting. We were all together and at last something had happened. And the fact [was] that Russia, which had stood always to all of us

radicals far more than the Turks, as the standard of despotism and reactionaries, had gone at last. We had no idea of the frightful state the Russian army was in. God knows how they managed to go on fighting. And nobody knew Lenin or the leaders. But of course we all knew Prince Kropotkin. We all knew Russian refugees. And they were all going back full of starry-eyed enthusiasm. This meeting was partly a send-off to those who were going back.

3 JUNE German forces reach the Marne, but the impetus of the attack is spent and the Allies, backed by fresh US troops, begin to push back

6 JUNE Independent Bombing Force, RAF, formed in order to promote an increase in strategic bombing

Prince Pyotr Alekseyovich Kropotkin, Russian revolutionary and foremost theorist of the anarchist movement.

Florence Farmborough was still in Russia as the country moved from the February revolution to the October Revolution and the takeover by Lenin and the Bolsheviks. It was at that time that the nurse from Buckinghamshire saw and heard the seventy-five-year-old aristocratic anarchist, Prince Kropotkin.

It was a most wonderful occasion. He was pronounced a revolutionary in imperial times, sent abroad, refused admittance to his country. But as a revolutionary he came back and, curiously enough, although the Russian Bolsheviki didn't agree with aristocrats and with titles, they accepted him.

On 6 April 1917, as the Russian Empire was in the throes of revolution, President Woodrow Wilson declared war on Germany. By the summer of 1917 the United States Army was arriving in France, and parts of it had passed

9-13 JUNE Battle of Noyon-Montdidier: Ludendorff launches another assault, threatening Paris and aiming to link his gains on the Somme with those in the Aisne-Marne sector. French defence halts the attack after some early gains, inflicting heavy losses on the Germans

15-22 JUNE An Anglo-French force of 5 divisions assists the Italian Army in the defence of the Piave River line. Strong counter-attacks, principally by the Italians, drive the Austro-Hungarian forces back with heavy casualties

through London. Munitionette **Caroline Rennles** found a new boyfriend.

> *I palled in with a German-American, come from Buffalo, New York. He went out to France — that was always happening. And one morning I says, 'Gather round, girls, I've just heard from Peter.'*
>
> *And he'd put in it, 'I love you, I love you, I love you, you are the most beautiful girl in the world'.*
>
> *They said: 'What's the matter with his eyesight?'*
>
> *'Now look,' I said, 'when an American says "You are the most beautiful girl", he must love me.'*

Emily Rumbold of the WAAC witnessed the arrival of Americans in Calais.

> *Some Americans stood near me. I think it was the day*

On the beach at Boulogne, US soldiers relax alongside British and French soldiers. (IWM: Q 10971)

> *after they had arrived in Calais. Ambulances were going down this very rough road; they took their hats off while the wounded went by, and if the wounded could possibly wave a foot or a hand they did so.*
>
> *And one of them said to me, 'I say, ma'am, weren't you down on the jetty yesterday when we came in?'*
>
> *I said, 'Well, there are many of us that are here but I did happen to be on the jetty — I went to see a friend of mine off.'*
>
> *They all looked and all of them would want to*

15 JULY-5 AUGUST Second Battle of the Marne: the fifth and last of the German offensives aims to secure the Marne river crossings, crushing a French army between two German. One attack is held by the French, but another breaks the line until held by French and US troops, with British and Italian forces in support. So ends the last major German offensive on the Western Front

US congressmen visit the Ordnance Works at Calais in 1917. (IWM: Q 3160)

fling their arms round your neck when they found that you could speak English because very few Americans could speak French.

Some of our men got rather fed up with girls going off with the Americans. They were paid far more than what our Tommies were. That was the trouble with the Australians too, you see – they had far more money than our troops. I think they used to get six shillings a day, or something like that, far more. Our men used to get seven shillings a week.

In spring 1918 the Germans launched their 'big push', which threw the Allies back to the lines of 1914 and the Marne. **Mairi Chisholm** was still in France – still on a nursing station, still driving, still with Mrs Elsie Knocker – and, in March 1918, was a casualty in the onslaught.

We were gassed with mustard and arsenic. Had it been pure mustard we should have been dead. We were the first cases to the Swiss specialist who was dealing in gas and he was frightfully intrigued with us because of the arsenic. But the arsenic has been a bother definitely, because it did your insides in for quite a long time for digestive purposes. The dog died – we had a terrier on the place for rats; the cat was very ill.

16 JULY–3 AUGUST General Foch, C-in-C of all Allied forces on the Western Front, goes back on to the attack, British, French US and Italian forces driving Ludendorff's armies back and retaking the salient won by the Germans in early June

8 AUGUST–3 SEPTEMBER Battle of Amiens: turning point of war on the Western Front. Foch's attack aims at driving the Germans out of the salient won by their gains on the Somme in March. As the battle ends all the German gains on the Somme have been retaken

The whole place went up – you couldn't hear yourself think. The whole line was one roar and it went on non-stop for forty-eight hours of intensive bombardment. You see our dugout – we had a pillbox where we slept in bunks, tiny, you could touch the walls all round, and the passageway from where we received the wounded to the dugout where we slept – had been entirely blown in with shellfire.

It was quite early in the morning; we had our gas masks on for about forty-eight hours. We were nearly dead with it because they pinched your nose hard, and you breathed through this tube which dribbled down your chest. We were sick of this. We pulled them off, and in that moment, practically, they lobbed in a salvo of gas shells into this broken-down passageway, which blew straight back into the pillbox, and was unpleasant.

The chemistry of horror: German soldiers adjust a line of gas throwers in 1917.

The horror: British soldiers are blinded by mustard gas, following an attack in France in April 1918.

The pillbox had the cut slanting slits for air, for ricochets of shell bits and pieces. We stuffed our Aquascutums into that, because the shell splinters were so frequent that they were coming from all directions. So we had no air in it, so we took a jolly good mouthful, and that was that. We were evacuated to hospital. The first thing I was wondering was whether we were going to ever see again, because our eyes were very badly taken with it. They put stuff in. The Swiss specialist was absolutely enchanted with us – he'd never had arsenic cases in before.

1918

12 SEPTEMBER Battle of St-Mihiel: the first great American triumph of the war. 16 US divisions, supported by the French, attack as the Germans begin to fall back in this sector, driving the enemy from the salient inside 36 hours

26 SEPTEMBER-11 NOVEMBER Battle of the River Meuse-Argonne Forest: US forces attack on a wide front in the south-east, in concert with other Allied attacks along the length of the Western Front. The Germans gradually fall back

27 SEPTEMBER-11 NOVEMBER Battle of Cambrai-St-Quentin: the western half of the great Allied attack, designed to trap the Germans in a pincer. By 4 October British, Canadian and French forces hold the entire German defensive position, and by the 31st the Germans have been driven back over the Scheldt River. The Allies prevent the enemy reinforcing against the French-US attack in the south-east, and early in November the Scheldt position is turned

CHAPTER SEVEN

ARMISTICE

MARSHAL LUDENDORFF CALLED 8 AUGUST 1918 the 'black day' of the German army. The British had advanced six miles into the German lines. By November the German Empire had followed its Russian, Austro-Hungarian and Ottoman counterparts into oblivion. At 11 a.m. on 11 November 1918 the exhausted Germans signed the Armistice.

Alongside the scourge of war was pestilence. The family of munitions worker

Caroline 'Queen' Rennles was one of millions affected worldwide.

My dad died two days before the Armistice. I loved my dad. He died with that terrible flu – shocking thing. On Armistice Day my mum had gone to register his

War is officially over. The Armistice is signed by the Germans in a railway carriage in the Forêt de Compiegne on 11 November 1918.

DISMISS

P. Moore

Standing to attention, a proud soldier is dismissed from his duties after the announcement of the Armistice.

death. They used to keep the bodies in the house then and my dad was laying in the front room in his coffin, and my mum had just had a little baby.

I heard the maroons go off and I thought it was another air raid, I didn't know about the Armistice, because we'd been up night and day with my dad with this terrific flu. I can remember running to the door with my little sister like my baby in my arms, and someone said, 'Oh, look at Queen.' I was so frightened that they ran over to me. I don't remember nothing about the Armistice really. I was in so much trouble.

I didn't stop work. We were lucky we knew an undertaker so that my dad was buried within about a

General Erich Ludendorff (right), who with Field Marshal Paul von Hindenburg (left) was responsible for Germany's military strategy and policy during the war, pictured with Kaiser Wilhelm II (centre). (IWM: Q 23746)

75

week or so, but some of the poor things was laying for two or three weeks. They couldn't bury them. They never had the men to make the coffins. I did hear that just by where my dad laid for his funeral they buried them in a pit.

By the time of the Armistice in 1918 **Mary Lees** had worked for the Land Army, trained Land Army recruits, managed a Land Army hostel – and in 1918 was working for the Air Ministry of the brand-new Royal Air Force in London.

Next door to us was the Ministry of Defence. And when the sirens went they threw a smoke bomb out of the window into Kingsway. And the first thing we knew was that Kingsway was packed out with fire engines. And the place was absolute bedlam. We'd all just been paid our wages. Well, we left them all on our desks. And we tore down the Strand. And the extraordinary thing was, before you could sneeze, there were thousands and thousands of tiny little Union Jacks everybody was holding. And we were carried in that crowd. If it hadn't been for a Frenchman in Trafalgar Square ... I mean it was packed so tight. This Frenchman was standing in front of me. I can remember seeing him now, he had a sort of flared coat on. And he suddenly put his head over his shoulder.

'Oh, my darling,' he said. 'Hold me tight. Put your arms on my waist and I'll keep you safe.'

Well, I put my hands on his waist. And we were carried right up to Oxford Circus in that

30 SEPTEMBER Bulgaria signs an armistice. Allied casualties in the Salonika campaign are 18,000 from battle, and 481,000 from malaria

24 OCTOBER-3 NOVEMBER Italian and Allied forces, after hard fighting, win crossings over the Piave and capture Vittorio Veneto. Austro-Hungarian resistance crumbles, and finally their forces are routed

Lilian Miles was still working in Buckingham's Bullet Factory when the siren went at 11 a.m.

We were doing our job, our bullets, in the factory. They came and told us earlier, about an hour before. They told us that the Armistice would be signed at eleven o'clock and that we have to stop work right away. We just stopped work and went home.

Ruby Ord was in France.

You thought about all the people you had known who were killed. They were just in the war zone, and they could come home in your imagination. But the Armistice brought the realization to you that they weren't coming back, that it was the end. It was not such a time of rejoicing as it might have been. We were glad the fighting was over and that not more men would be killed but it was dampened down very much, in France. I did not go out of camp on Armistice Day.

The Prime Minister, David Lloyd George, had called the General Election for Saturday 14 December 1918. On 6 February of that year

They had survived; Scots and Australian soldiers in London's Strand with a WAAC member on Armistice Day.

David Lloyd George, British Prime Minister (1916-22), who, in 1918, called a General Election in which women over thirty could vote for the first time. (IWM: Q 70208)

crowd. It was quite terrifying. We had a frightfully snooty sort of boss at the office. He was a sort of Air Vice-Marshal. We all disliked him enormously. And the final thing we saw going down the Strand that day was the boss sitting on the top of a taxi with his arm round the youngest messenger girl.

30 OCTOBER Turkey signs an armistice

3 NOVEMBER Austria-Hungary signs an armistice

8 NOVEMBER A German armistice delegation secretly crosses the Allied line under a white flag, and meets Foch and his Allied advisers to discuss terms of surrender. Further north, Belgian forces drive the Germans out of Ostend, Zeebrugge and Bruges

1918

Armistice celebrations in London's Piccadilly Circus.

Women aged thirty years or more vote for the first time in December 1918.

Parliament had granted the right to vote to women who were householders, or married to householders, or university graduates, over the age of thirty. Ten years later the right was extended to women over the age of twenty-one, placing them – in this area at least – on an equal footing with men. **Jane Cox**:

When we got the vote – and I admired Mrs Pankhurst – I said, 'I'll never neglect to vote.' I always voted. The war allowed women to stand on their

10 NOVEMBER Kaiser Wilhelm II of Germany abdicates and flees to exile in neutral Holland, where he dies in 1941

11 NOVEMBER The Armistice is signed at 5 a.m., to take effect at 11 a.m. – 'the eleventh hour of the eleventh day of the eleventh month'. It is greeted in Britain with displays ranging from the quietly joyful and relieved to the downright riotous

Women bricklayers prepare the site for the building of a new aeroplane production shop in Birmingham. Caroline Rennles protested against the fact that many women workers would be losing their jobs as the war ended. (IWM: Q 109787)

own feet. It was the turning point. Men became a little bit humbler. They weren't the bosses any more. Years ago, once you were married, you stopped at home. The men could go down the pub but the woman couldn't. But during the war women learned.

In the 1918 election – her war hero father was returned as a Liberal MP again – **Helen**

Pease was campaigning in Hanley, in the Potteries.

One of the vast crowd of what they called hard-faced men won. And then when we all saw the sort of crew we'd got in the government, well, I joined the Independent Labour Party. It was obvious the Liberals were no earthly, they were absolutely tied hand and foot to the hard-faced men.

Dorothy Bing, who, like her father and brother, had been a staunch pacifist throughout the war, attempted to heal a breach with her mother's relatives who had lost a son on the Western Front.

I was teaching in Catford where they lived. I went purposely, after the war was over. It was terribly

21 NOVEMBER The German Imperial High Seas Fleet sails out to internment and demilitarization at the British Home Fleet's base at Scapa Flow, Orkney Islands

14 DECEMBER Women over 30 years old who are householders, the wives of householders, occupiers of property with an annual rent of £5 or more, or graduates of British universities have their first opportunity to vote in a General Election

1918

hurtful to my mother. Two sisters, the two who were nearest to her, just wouldn't have anything to do with her – or any of us for that matter. And they just looked at me – no, nothing came at all. Mother was very loyal to her husband and her son and I think she suffered a great deal though and she died when she was sixty-one, which was fairly young for her family; most of them lived longer. She never said much about it but I'm quite sure it was a dreadful blow to her that she was cut off from her family. I was never very sure to what extend she really agreed. She was a housewife, pure and simple. Very fond of her home and proud of her children but not of a philosophical nature particularly. Brought up quite conventionally. She remained absolutely loyal; I think it did have very bad effect on her.

For **Caroline Rennles** the end of the war was the end of work.

They put us down breaking up the bullets and then they threw us all out on the slag heap. We walked to the Houses of Parliament, protesting that we'd been thrown out. It must have been two or three thousand – walked over the bridge and we went right up to the door of the Houses of Parliament and before you could say Jack Robinson, there was hundreds of policemen on horseback dispersing us. And I saw one little Irish girl who was with us – she pulled the reins down from this horse – but we run for our life, we all run down the Embankment.

In France **Emily Rumbold** watched as some soldiers revolted.

The regimental sergeant-major – who was hated – gave the order to right turn and not a soul moved. They said it was worth going in for to see just the expression on his face, he looked so horrified because nobody had said a word to him about it. They'd not said a word to the girls about going on this strike, they said it was no good; the girls would only give it away.

And after a day or two, some of us went on down to the depot just to say we weren't going on strike, and then Major Marfleet said, 'You must clear out, and go over the roadway, not through the

1914-1918 THE COST Great Britain, the Dominions and the British Empire lost 908,371 servicemen killed during the First World War, with another 2,090,212 wounded and 191,652 captured or missing, a total of 3,190, 235 casualties in all. More than 700,000 of the dead were from the UK.

In addition, 1,274 British civilians were killed and 3,121 injured in air raids by Zeppelins and Gotha bombers, 1915-18; in 1916 and 1917, which saw the heaviest bombing of Britain, 906 civilians were killed and 2,182 injured

1918

depot because there are a hundred men marching down here to throw out the girls who are working.'

By 1919 **Mary Rumney**, the society girl of 1914, had been a nurse, and a sister from Colchester to Salonika and Serbia. She had served in the army and the navy, and worked with the Canadian army.

I was quite sorry when it was over. I was going back to the leisured classes. A parlour maid and a cook and a gardener and so on. My brother dead. The other brother at a lovely school and the little sister growing up. Oh no. And mother – not pleased to see me.

For **Ruby Ord** her army career counted for nothing.

It was very difficult if you had been a WAAC. We weren't looked upon with favour by the people at home. We had done something that was outrageous for women to do. We had gone to France and left our homes. We had quite a job getting fixed up.

For **Dorothy Bing**, pacifist, the war had changed everything.

The idea that women could do men's jobs undermined the whole idea of society. No woman who married expected to go out to work. Not even the working-class women. Their job was to stay at home and have child after child after child. I mean ten, eleven, twelve children was nothing. My father came eight or nine, I think, from the mother of ten children. So that the woman hadn't an earthly. She was either pregnant or nursing a child.

Caroline Rennles's distrust of Germans remained.

We hated them more or less, didn't we? But a chap I knew, he married a German girl, oh, she was lovely. She used to say to me, 'Look, Queen, your men had to fight and our men had to fight, they had to go.'

Well, of course they had to go, but it's stupid, war, don't you think so? Where are we now? There's all those lovely boys been killed and we're worse off than we've ever been, aren't we? Can't get a room, can't get nothing. So, what's the good of war, love?

A war cemetery near the Church of Villers aux Bois, Pas de Calais, France. (IWM: Q 69683)

British nurses at a hospital in the Balkans care for Serbian patients. (IWM: Q 107355)

1914-18 SUMMARY Before the war, the female workforce in Britain numbered some 200,000 women, most of them in the textile industries. By the war's end, more than 5 million women are engaged in 1,071 different kinds of work formerly done by men. The social effects to the country are profound, but one of the most positive is the granting of the right to vote to women over 30

1918

CHAPTER EIGHT

THE DIRTY DECADE

WOMEN AT WAR, POST-WAR, MIGHT BE DENIED employment, but they could not be denied some of their rights. In 1923 the Matrimonial Causes Act gave women equal grounds for divorce. In 1928 Great Britain finally became a parliamentary democracy when the Equal Franchise Act gave all women over twenty-one the vote. But a year later the Wall Street Crash ushered in the 'dirty decade' of totalitarian aggression.

In 1919, at Versailles, the leaders of the victorious nations of the First World War had imposed on Germany a peace settlement that helped ensure the resumption of hostilities twenty years later. The 1920s were poisoned by arguments about the 'reparations' to be paid by democratic Germany. The 1930s were consumed by the consequences of the Treaty's failure: Adolf Hitler's regime in Germany, Benito Mussolini's fascist regime in Italy, the

Making new war from peace: in a painting by Sir William Orpen, heads of state sign the Treaty of Versailles in the Hall of Mirrors on 28 June 1919. (IWM: ART 2856)

Evil begets greater evil: Germany's President von Hindenburg, First World War general, with Adolf Hitler, whom Hindenburg appointed Chancellor in January 1933.

invasion of China by Japan. In the 1930s opinion was sharply divided between those who saw Joseph Stalin's Soviet Union as the light of the world, and those who saw it as a totalitarian nightmare.

Faced with what had happened in the years 1914–18, some women joined organizations like the League of Nations Union, the No More War Movement, the Women's International League for Peace and Freedom, and, in the 1930s, the Peace Pledge Union. But alongside revulsion against war, came another conviction – the inevitability of war.

In the beginning, however, the idea that Hitler would come to power still seemed, to some, unlikely. At Christmas 1932 **Margareta Burkill**, Berlin-born Russian and British-educated, was a twenty-four-year-old on holiday with her family in

European allies: Adolf Hitler meets Italian Fascist leader Benito Mussolini in Venice. (IWM: HU 3640)

Switzerland.

> We were skiing in Arosa and we met Ernst Reuter, who ultimately became Mayor of Berlin, who was then head of the railways in Berlin. He was a socialist member of the Reichstag who had been a pupil of my father's. We asked him, 'What about the Nazi business?'
>
> He said, 'Oh, that'll be all right, the economics of Germany are improving, it will disappear.'
>
> By March 1933 Ernst Reuter was in a concentration camp; it was one of the real shocks.

Burkill's success in getting Reuter and his son out of Germany was to open a new chapter in her life.

Nearly two decades on from teaching in South Shields, **Isabel Brown** was heavily involved in British Communist politics, and visiting Germany.

> I spoke at meetings because, as a hangover from the 1914–18 war there was still antagonism, hatred of the Germans as Germans, not selecting who were the warmongers. And we wanted to try and break this feeling. So we used to have a peace day on August 4, the first day of the First World War. And I always went as our representative there to speak because,

1919 Spanish influenza pandemic finally abates in the UK. In all, 237,400 people have died from the 'flu in Britain since it first struck in early 1918

18 JANUARY 1919 Paris Peace Conference. The Treaty of Versailles, signed 28 June 1919, ends the war with Germany; others signed in 1919 and 1920 deal with Austria, Bulgaria, Hungary and Turkey (the latter was never adopted, and was superseded by

being young, fresh and vigorous, I made a good impression. I spoke in the election campaign when Hindenburg won the election and invited Hitler to become the Chancellor, which was early in 1933. And our side had the famous – which became infamous – Sportpalast; the biggest hall in Berlin was crowded out. I was one of the speakers at the last democratic meeting held during the election campaign, at the end of which Hitler became Chancellor.

In 1935 sixteen-year old **Brigitte Davies** was at school in Berlin. Her parents were German, her mother of German-Jewish origin. One day her teacher set an essay title for the class: 'What is a Hero?'

I had a friend whose father was a minister in the Christian church. And he later belonged to a church which was opposed to the Nazis. But at this time he had refused to give the oath as ministers of the church were required to do. And I chose to write my essay about this father of my friend saying: 'That to me is a hero, a man who refuses for his beliefs to make such an oath. And yet he realized, and must have realized the consequences – that from then onwards he couldn't support his children any more.'

And great exception was taken to this because it was my friend in my form – a woman with whom I've remained friendly to this day.

She was thrown out of the school. In March 1939, she arrived in Britain. Year by year the European situation had deteriorated.

In the spring of 1936 Hitler reoccupied the Rhineland. A pattern was set. That July the Spanish army officer Francisco Franco landed

in mainland Spain, and led the Fascist revolt against the Spanish republic. **Isabel Brown** began fundraising for Spain.

Put me up to ask for money for wounded men, and, my God, we got it. The first meeting we had in the Albert Hall, a professor from France came, a famous one. Paul Robeson spoke and sang. And we got over two thousand pounds at that first meeting. And then we had little meetings. I spoke with Jack [J. B.] Priestley in Bradford, his home town. The biggest hall in Bradford was crammed.

From meetings and money in England she took the train to Republican-held Barcelona.

We were going through villages, and the only protection for the village was a load of hay, a little way across the road and then a gap and another load there. And a boy about fourteen with an old hunting gun guarding the village. That, to me, was tragic.

In April 1937 aircraft of the Nazi Condor Legion, assisted by Italian fliers, wiped out

US actor and singer Paul Robeson (centre), pictured with American International Brigaders in Madrid. He spoke and sang at a fundraising event for the Spanish republic organized by Isabel Brown. (IWM: HU 34730)

another treaty in 1923). The 'Great War' is over; however, the measures forced upon Germany by the Treaty foreshadow a second and even more terrible war

21 JUNE 1919 Skeleton crews on the German ships interned at Scapa Flow open the sea cocks to scuttle their vessels. Most are sunk. Work on raising the major vessels begins in 1924, but is not completed until 1946

1919

the town of Guernica in the Basque Country. The town became a symbol of the horror of fascism, and aerial warfare. **Isabel Brown**:

> The phrase I used in making appeals for support for Republican Spain was, 'It is Guernica today, it will be Paris, London, Coventry tomorrow if we don't defeat the Franco crowd.'

She helped organize the evacuation of Basque children for the duration of the war. They were put up in a camp outside Southampton.

> Those little girls and boys coming out, nice clipped hair, girls' hair curled up, in beautiful new clothes,

General Francisco Franco, leader of the right-wing nationalists who overthrew the Spanish republic in the civil war (1936-39) and established a dictatorship which lasted until 1975.

Republican militiamen, pictured with a local girl near the Aragon Front, in 1936.
(IWM: HU 32986)

JULY 1919 Huge Victory Parade in London; the women's services, which now include Queen Alexandra's Royal Army Nursing Corps (QARANC) and the Field Auxiliary Nursing Yeomanry (FANY), take part, as do volunteer nursing and other organizations

1 DECEMBER 1920 Nancy, Lady Astor, becomes the first woman MP to take her seat in the House of Commons, having succeeded to her husband's seat on his inheriting his father's title

Basque children who fled Spain during the civil war are looked after in England, 1938. (IWM: HU 33135)

was a sight that made many of us weep with joy that at least we'd taken them out of the war area. I'd been living in Northumberland during the 1914–18 war and knew nothing about bombing. But those Basque children had known it. And the first evening, just as it was coming dusk, some aeroplanes came over. We had a near panic in the camp. Thank God there were a number of Spaniards, teachers and priests that could help to calm the situation.

In September 1938 the British Prime Minister Neville Chamberlain, after effectively

granting Adolf Hitler the right to dismember Czechoslovakia, returned to Britain promising 'peace with honour'. Twenty-five-year-old pacifist **Doris Nicholls** was a member of the London committee of the Fellowship of Reconciliation. She was delighted that the Prime Minister had apparently rescued peace from war. Then she heard an address by another pacifist, Alan Balding, later the Master of Christ's College Cambridge.

We learnt at a conference of the Fellowship of Reconciliation because of the wisdom of one of the clergy, who was, I think, a very great man, that there was a considerable difference between appeasement and reconciliation, that the two words did not mean the same thing. And I can still recall the shock it was for me, to be forced to think through that one.

22 JANUARY 1924 The first Labour government of Great Britain takes office under Ramsay MacDonald

4-13 MAY 1926 The TUC calls a General Strike of heavy-industry workers, with sympathetic strikes by male and female workers in other industries. Troops and volunteers, including women, help run essential services, and the strike only lasts 9 days

1926

Daily Herald

No. 7061   SATURDAY, OCTOBER 1, 1938   ONE PENNY

MR. CHAMBERLAIN DECLARES "IT IS PEACE FOR OUR TIME"

5,000 British Troops Will Be Sent To Sudetenland

PRAGUE'S DAY OF SORROW

To a frenzied welcome from tens of thousands of Londoners, Mr. Neville Chamberlain came home last night and announced to all the world: "I believe it is peace for our time."

GERMANS   The Premier had two agreements in his pocket: 1.—The Munich Four-Power Pact for the transfer of

From a Window at No. 10

BUT—
Poles Rush Ultimatum

BY OUR OWN CORRESPONDENT
WARSAW, Friday night.

WITHIN 24 hours of one threat of an immediate war on the Czechs being averted, Poland tonight handed a new ultimatum to Prague.

Imposing a 24-hour time limit, the ultimatum insisted on an immediate answer to the demand that all Czech territory inhabited by Poles shall be evacuated at once.

A Warsaw Foreign Office spokesman announced that the Note would reach Prague by ten o'clock to-night. An official communiqué explained that Czechoslovakia's answer to the Polish Note, sent last Tuesday, containing a detailed plan of frontier adjustments in Teschen Silesia, reached Warsaw at 1 p.m. to-day, but had been found unsatisfactory.

The Polish Government had therefore sent another Note requesting a "clear and precise" answer and the cession of the territory.

The answer to the Note is expected "will resort to measures which may have the gravest consequences."

Suggestions were made that Polish troops would enter the Teschen district of Czechoslovakia to-morrow at the same time that the Germans occupied the areas ceded to them.

The official wireless broadcast a message from Teschen which declared: "The hour is approaching when Polish troops will free the Poles in Czechoslovakia with their fixed bayonets."

Reports were circulated in Warsaw to-day of alleged "incidents" on the Czech border.

An urgent meeting was called, attended by General Smigly-Rydz, virtual Dictator of Poland, President Moscicki, the Premier, vice-Premier and Foreign Minister.

Hitler's terror campaign within Germany, and his anti-Semitic outrages accelerated. On what became known as Kristallnacht – the Night of (Broken) Glass – 9-10 November 1938, gangs of Nazi youths destroyed 101 synagogues and more than 7,000 Jewish businesses. Some 26,000 Jews were sent to concentration camps, and 91 died as a consequence of that night. By then **Margareta Burkill** was a leading member of the Cambridge Refugee Committee.

> Kristallnacht went through Great Britain like a sort of electric current, every little town, every village in England said, 'We must save the children.' It was quite a fantastic thing, people who'd never thought about the Nazis or anything else but when they heard about this murder and burning that was the reaction.
>
> The Home Office agreed that a suitable

A good idea at the time? The Labour-supporting *Daily Herald* was among the papers hoping for the best after Prime Minister Neville Chamberlain's Munich talks with Hitler.

> committee could bring in ten thousand unaccompanied children. Within nine months, before the beginning of the war, we had brought out just under ten thousand and we would have made our permission of ten thousand if one trainload from Czechoslovakia hadn't been stopped in Germany on the day the war was declared.

By the end of March 1939 Franco had won the Spanish civil war. It was **Isabel Brown's** task that August to join a British National Joint Relief lorry sent to the Franco-Spanish border to succour the disarmed Republican soldiers.

7 MAY 1928 The voting age for women is lowered to 21, the franchise for women finally coming into line with that for men

16 MAY 1936 The Women's Voluntary Service (WVS) is established. By 1942 it has some 2 million women members, and is involved in the evacuation of children and providing welfare services to the armed forces, refugees and bombing victims

It was a beautiful stretch of golden, golden sands just north on the coast near Perpignan just above Port Bou on the blue beautiful Mediterranean, beautiful blue sky. But the men were mostly in the water because they had not any shelter. And they had dug underground in the soft sand and tried to shore them up with whatever material they could get. They gathered up shells and little bits of rock. That was the only shelter they had from the blazing sun of the Mediterranean.

We stood on this lorry and we had to pick up the parcels and call out a name and give it to whoever came and got it. And I watched one wounded soldier dragging through the sand to get away from the sun and [he] crawled under the lorry that we had put our parcels on. And his name wasn't on the list. And the look of disappointment! I'll never forget that picture.

Less than a month later, the Second World War began.

Spanish Republican soldiers retreat along the coast road to France, January 1939. (IWM: HU 33166)

1938 The Auxiliary Territorial Service (ATS) is established by former members of the WAAC, which was disbanded at the end of the First World War

SEPTEMBER 1938 British Prime Minister Neville Chamberlain visits Germany three times to prevent the outbreak of a European war over Hitler's demand that Czechoslovakia cede the Sudetenland to Germany

CHAPTER NINE

THE OUTBREAK

IN 1938, AT THE TIME OF THE MUNICH CRISIS some thirty-eight million gas masks were issued to the British people. Soon afterwards four-year-old **Sylvia Townson** was given her present by the government.

I had a Mickey Mouse gas mask. I believe it had black ears. I don't think it worried me too much, I tried it on, I remember being taught how to wear it. I think, after that, it just went into a box.

A year later, on 3 September 1939, the Prime Minister, Neville Chamberlain, addressed the people of Great Britain, and told them that the country was at war with Germany. One of

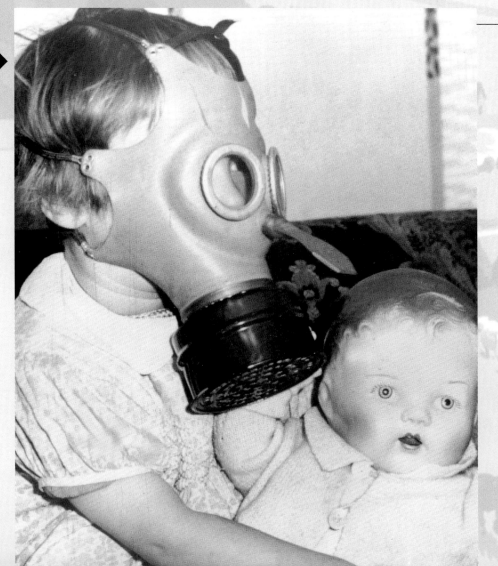

A little girl wears a brightly coloured gas mask, specially made for toddlers.
(IWM: HU 33355)

Neville Chamberlain announces the outbreak of war in a radio broadcast.

the people listening to the broadcast was **Nan Kenway**. Born in New South Wales, by the 1930s she was an entertainer in Britain. That summer she was performing in Cornwall.

We were in Newquay with a concert party. And we listened, as many of us did, to those dreadful words on the radio that 'we are now at war with Germany'. And the first cat out of the bag affected us deeply. Because they said, 'All places of entertainment will now close.' Mmm, it was a bit of a death knell to us. After all, it was our livelihood.

Yvonne Cormeau was twenty-nine, recently married, with a small child, and working in London.

I can't say it was a surprise. We could see with friends and relations living abroad that things were

building up, and being able to listen to certain speeches I could understand that something was going to happen indeed. It seemed to me the only way we could honourably stand up to our promises.

Josephine Pearce, a nurse, was organizing evacuees.

I was standing on a rural bridge admiring the trout. And I heard somebody's wireless, through one of their cottage windows, when Chamberlain was announcing that war was declared, that we were now at war with Germany. And the whole bottom fell out of one's life.

Born in France, of English parents, soon after she was on her way to France.

London had the atmosphere of war when we came

away. I remember coming out of Holborn station and we couldn't see a thing, because blackout was blackout, and touching a gentleman – I could just see him in the gloom – and asking him where the bus to wherever it was I was going went from. And he said, 'Oh, I'll take you there.'

And there was a dim light in the bus. And I saw that it was a black man who had very courteously taken me. And I remember sitting on the bus and thinking, 'Good gracious, he was black.' Well, we weren't used to black people much in England.

By the end of 1939 **Josephine Pearce** had arrived in Paris on her way to join Ambulance Unit 282, with the French army in Alsace.

The atmosphere in Paris ... was not the Paris I knew. There was something. I remember going to visit a

1 SEPTEMBER After softening-up air bombardments and supported by aircraft, German troops invade Poland

2 SEPTEMBER German troops and armour, supported by aircraft, advance across Poland; British Cabinet sends Germany an ultimatum

great friend of mine in a top-floor flat in the Avenue Bosquet. But I remember her friend saying to me in French, 'They talk of peace, my dear, what peace? We've been sold. Nous sommes vendus.' And it didn't register too much at the time. But when I eventually got up to Sarraguemines, where the unit was, and inundated with questions from the nurses, I remember them asking me: 'Was Paris behaving itself?'

And at first I thought, 'What do they mean?'

I realized what they meant because we'd been at war for three months. And they were behaving as though there was no war. They were doing nothing, nothing to protect the people, nothing to protect themselves. And that was what Madame meant. 'We're sold. Nous sommes vendus.' What peace? She knew. She could foresee.

Police in steel helmets control a crowd gathered in Downing Street, cheering at the news of the declaration of war. (IWM: HU 36164)

Standing by their belongings, children wait with a nurse, ready for evacuation.

3 SEPTEMBER Hitler ignores the ultimatum, leading Britain and France to make an official declaration of war against Germany; Prime Minister Chamberlain informs the British people that 'a state of war now exists between Great Britain and Germany'

10 SEPTEMBER Headed by General Lord Gort, the first large units of the BEF embark for France

17 SEPTEMBER Soviet troops invade Poland

1939

CHAPTER TEN

NOWHERE TO RUN

THE BOMBING OF GUERNICA, FOLLOWING ON from Japanese bombing in China and Italian gas attacks in Abyssinia, chilled the western world. In 1939–40 the British anticipated high explosives and gas cascading from the sky. Official evacuation began on 1 September 1939, as the Nazis invaded Poland. But between June and September almost four million people had moved to 'safe' areas; however, in the initial months of the 'phoney war' the evacuees returned. As the threat turned – without gas – to reality, waves of evacuation ebbed and flowed. The 'people', rich, poor and in between, were finally forced to face each other. The results were heartening – and horrifying. Many children were forced to make long journeys, but for four-year-old Marylebone-born **Sylvia Townson** it was just a trip to Buckinghamshire.

> *I remember getting off the train in High Wycombe and standing on the platform, being pushed into some kind of crocodile, and walking from the station in the middle of the road, again in a great column and taken to a reception centre, and people standing on the pavements. I wasn't sure what they*

were saying at the time, I wasn't taking very much notice at that age. I was probably more aware of the people walking with me. But my mother did tell me afterwards that people were shouting quite a lot of abuse, calling us foreigners and refugees. They probably didn't want a great influx of Londoners into somewhere as suburban and select as High Wycombe in those days. So I think it wasn't very pleasant for the people arriving there.

In 1940 Exmouth-born **Nancy Bazin** was eighteen years old and teaching in the West Country.

In that first evacuation the children were carrying little cardboard suitcases that used to be the sort of thing that you could buy in Woolworth's. I remember one child, a little boy of about five, his suitcase was just packed with comics. These little things with their gas-mask box and a little suitcase in their

Evacuation was a vast logistical problem and women made it work. (IWM: PST 5873)

CIVIL DEFENCE

WOMEN WANTED FOR EVACUATION SERVICE

OFFER YOUR SERVICES TO YOUR LOCAL COUNCIL

OR ANY BRANCH OF WOMEN'S VOLUNTARY SERVICES

Blitzkrieg: German tanks in Poland.

hands looked dejected, very small children in particular. And we were taking them to homes with people speaking in, to their way, a very curiously different accent.

The Devonian is a kind-hearted person, but on the other hand not very used to the Cockney child. In most cases they settled in very well, particularly in the completely rural areas because there the farm children had a great plus in that they knew everything about the animals and the livestock and the general countryside, and there was a lot of interest for the town children. Though they felt unfamiliar they weren't uninterested in suddenly being surrounded by a lot of animals, and children who could teach them so much.

In London children leave the dangers of the city for the relative safety of the countryside. (IWM: AP 7455B)

The children who were from Lambeth, and Elephant and Castle and some of the really fairly deprived areas of London, were keen, alert Cockney minds, frequently very good at the sort of things you'd expect they might be good at – mental arithmetic and things which the Devon child probably was much slower in. I was teaching in these schools all in fairly rural situations on the fringe of Dartmoor. The children were billeted in farm labourers' cottages or on the farms and in many cases with very old people who were remarkably kind.

1939

29 SEPTEMBER Under the secret pre-war Nazi-Soviet Pact, Germany and Soviet Union partition Poland between them

22 DECEMBER 'Munitionettes' demand the same wages as their male co-workers

28 DECEMBER Meat rationing introduced in Britain

German tactics
exposed Anglo-French
failings. This was a
French Air Force hangar
after a visit from Stuka
dive bombers.
(IWM: MH 1931)

London children await
evacuation.
(IWM: TP 7089)

1 JANUARY 2 million 19–27-year-olds in Britain are called up to join the war effort; the first 8 women pilots of the Air Transport Auxiliary (ATA) enter service. The ATA employs experienced civilian pilots, including women, to ferry new and replacement aircraft to squadrons of the RAF and Fleet Air Arm. By the war's end, ATA pilots (150 women in all, and about 4 times that number of men) had moved 309,011 aircraft of 140 types

By May 1940 the Germans, having completed their initial dismemberment of Poland, had turned their attentions to the west. Their Blitzkrieg was splitting France in two. The situation of **Josephine Pearce** in Alsace, attached to the French Fourth Army was becoming desperate. Her ambulance unit 282 headed south.

France was just one mass of different regiments, different generals, hither and thither, none knowing what the other was doing. And it wasn't until we got into the Champagne territory that we began to realize that we were retreating, that it was quite obvious that we would never set up hospital again, that we were running away. Sometimes we got proper instructions, and when we got to where we were told to go, they had gone. And it was constantly so. We were going to set up a hospital here. They'd gone. We were going to set up a hospital there. They'd gone. In the end we found no one and we realized we were on our own. And we must do what we could on our own.

8 JANUARY Wide food-rationing regulations introduced in Britain for the first time since 1918: butter, bacon, sugar and ham can only be bought with a ration book

9 APRIL Germany invades Norway: major Norwegian ports occupied by advance detachments of German troops. Simultaneously, German troopships, covered by aircraft, enter Copenhagen harbour as Denmark becomes occupied territory

In Britain **Nancy Bazin** observed the deteriorating situation with alarm. Between 27 May and 4 June 338,226 troops were evacuated from Dunkirk. It was the end of the British Expeditionary Force in France.

Our ships were being sunk, our convoys were losing ships, some of our major battleships were lost, our aircraft were taking a pounding. The evacuation of France, and Dunkirk, gave us an amazing amount of morale boost, but when you consider it was a terrible defeat, it was turned into an amazing situation because so many people survived. But of course it was a terrible defeat and it really brought the Germans that much nearer. Now they were really looking at us just across that little stretch of water. We were up against it and we were alone.

Josephine Pearce and the other twenty-five members of her medical unit were alone, and still in France. Units of the French and British armies continued to fight. On 22 June 1940 France signed an armistice with

The evacuation from Dunkirk – the disaster from which the British plucked success – and created an heroic myth. (IWM: ART LD 305)

Marshal Pétain, First World War hero who became head of France's collaborationist pro-Hitler government from 1940 until 1944.

10 MAY Winston Churchill becomes British Prime Minister as Neville Chamberlain resigns after the débâcle of the Allied intervention in Norway; he forms a war cabinet from the main political parties; German invasion of Holland and Belgium begins

12 MAY German forces cross the Franco-Belgian frontier and begin their advance across France; outclassed and outmanoeuvred, British and French forces fall back, often in confusion

1940

Hundreds of refugees lined the roads to Dunkirk. (IWM: HU 2284)

Members of the First Aid Nursing Yeomanry (FANY) run to their ambulances.

Germany, and Marshal Pétain set up his collaborationist government in Vichy.

Then we were the enemy. We were on our own. And if it hadn't been for the medical orderlies, medical students, staying with us, and the médecin chef Dr Gosset, staying with us as long as they did, I think we would have been taken prisoner. They stayed with us as far into the south of France as they could possibly stay. And in that way we managed to get petrol, until came the day when we were siphoning petrol from one car, one van or one lorry into the next car, all the time saying, 'But where are our own soldiers? Where is our air force? Why aren't they here?'

We were still not understanding what was happening in France. All these refugees on the roads. What was happening? After the [Pétain] armistice, we knew that we were the enemy. And the most dreadful thing to us was that as we passed through villages, they would throw flowers at us thinking we were the British, coming to save them. That was the state that France was in. Nobody knew what was happening at all. This was organized chaos, very well organized chaos by the enemy.

The chaos did not extend to everybody. The members of the medical unit came off the Plateau Central, and went up into the hills,

away from the refugee columns.

There was an old man and his son. We discovered them one day with a great tree right across the road. They were protecting France. We weren't to go by till we'd shown our papers. One old man and one little boy, one gun. And he inspected all our papers. And that was France. Real France.

Sleeping in barns and ditches, the twenty-six women made their way on towards Bordeaux.

You felt so futile when you saw a granny hugging a baby that was absolutely dead, sitting on top of a cart piled up with furniture and being machine-gunned. And the baby had got the bullet. And the granny swaying backwards and forwards with the baby, holding it to protect it. And she didn't know she was protecting a dead baby. One saw so much that was utterly unbelievable.

They made Bordeaux, and via the Royal Navy and a passenger ship, back to England, and, for an exhausted party, an unwelcome enthusiastic reception from Fleet Street. The missing unit had been headline news in the British press.

In the wake of Dunkirk and the fall of France, the British were waiting for the Germans.

1940

15 MAY Holland surrenders to Germany

26 MAY Order is issued for Operation Dynamo – evacuation of the British Expeditionary Force and of French troops from the port and beaches at Dunkirk

28 MAY Belgium surrenders to the Nazis

4 JUNE Completion of Operation Dynamo – over 337,000 Allied troops are rescued; Churchill makes his rousing 'We shall fight them on the beaches' speech

Nancy Bazin:

We were told that we had to mobilize all our civilian force in Exmouth to resist the invasion that was likely to come across the Channel. Our local battalion of Devons which were organizing this were going round with microphones and loud speakers, calling us to come to the beach with spades and shovels, anything we could lay our hands on. And I with several friends, I remember particularly the stretch of sand allotted; it was very near where our lifeboat station was. We were told to dig, and we dug a trench in the sand, and we were, at the same time as digging, and getting blisters on our hands, and working for hours on this, we were looking out to sea expecting to see these flotillas of German invading troops come. On this whole two-mile stretch of beach we were digging this trench, and it

was so obviously hopeless because, with the wind and the rain and the high tide, all our work would disappear. But we did it, in this extraordinary way, believing that somehow we were defending. That was a futile operation. There was a sergeant or an officer every hundred yards saying 'Keep digging.'

She had given up teaching and joined the First Aid Nursing Yeomanry (FANY) as a driver.

These people trained us and they had such a spirit of service and of the way in which your duty lay, that it was imbued into us. I must have been eighteen and a half, something like that, and very much feeling that this was the way we were going to save Britain, by our determination and the great cause that we were all involved in. I suppose that was true of every young person joining up at that time. We weren't frightened,

10 JUNE Italy declares war on the Allies; Germany completes its occupation of Norway

14 JUNE German troops enter Paris

16 JUNE As German forces advance through France Marshal Pétain, the hero of Verdun in 1916 and recently appointed head of the French government, proposes an armistice to Germany

1940

we were worried, we were just determined that here we were, this little island, fighting against tremendous odds with the whole of the world outside to cope with – in that at the time there was no question of the Americans coming into the war – and we were alone and yet here we were battling, with all our menfolk going overseas to take the front line, and we the women filling in where we could to take their jobs. That was a pretty general feeling, not being frightened, but being determined we were doing the right thing.

A recruitment poster for the Women's Auxiliary Air Force (WAAF). (IWM: PST 3096)

After Dunkirk, and the decision of the British to fight on, the Germans launched their daylight attacks on Britain, with the aim of destroying the Royal Air Force as an essential prelude to any invasion. Among the crucial weapons available to the British was the network of radar stations that ringed the south coast and provided early warning of the arrival of the Luftwaffe. Increasingly it was women who took over the key roles in tracking the movements of the enemy aircraft.

In the late 1930s **Anne Duncan** had ambitions of becoming a dress designer after completing art school. But with the threat of war in 1939 she had sought to join the FANY. She was turned down as she didn't have a car – although she did get a flying licence after five pounds' worth of lessons near Southampton. So, late in 1939, she had joined the WAAF, and was trained as a plotter at Leighton Buzzard.

We were billeted in a beautiful country house. The first day going into it we were absolutely fascinated because it was all covered with camouflage over the top. We couldn't think why but we realized then that it must be something very secret. There were all these huts and things where we were taught. There was a table with a map of England on it and the whole of the map was marked out in a grid. The man on the other end of the telephone, when he was reporting things coming in, he'd give you two letters and four numbers and from that you put down a little round disc like a tiddlywink. Then a few minutes later there would be another one – that would be a bit further on and you could see the course gradually building up of something coming in. You plotted everything. Everything came in over the radar tubes and the problem was to decide which was friendly and which was not. It was quite easy in the beginning because anything that was friendly went from England outwards and anything that was not came from France or Holland and Belgium inwards.

1940

17 JUNE Churchill delivers his 'Finest hour' speech

22 JUNE France capitulates and signs an armistice with Germany

10 JULY The Luftwaffe bombs military targets in southern England, testing the RAF's response. This signals the start of the Battle of Britain, which Germany views as a precursor to invasion, while Britain sees it as a last stand against conquest

In a painting by Charles Ernest Cundall, WAAFs place aircraft on a map table and chalk up aircraft positions in the Operations Room of No 11 Fighter Group, Uxbridge. (IWM: ART LD 4140)

That summer the Battle of Britain erupted over the skies of southern England. **Vera Holdstock** was an eighteen-year-old member of the Women's Land Army. Her Italian father, headwaiter at the Savoy Hotel in London, had become a British citizen in the wake of Mussolini's conquest of Abyssinia. In 1940 Vera had just arrived on her first farm near Tenterden in Kent – where one of her friends came from a German-English

background. Above her head was the Battle of Britain.

We had a first-class view. They used to have dogfights over the farm and we found it most exciting. We didn't realize the danger. We used to stand open-mouthed and watch it all. One night one of the sheds on the farm was set alight by incendiary bombs. I think the Germans were just going back over the Channel and they just unloaded their bombs on the way back. We had some blue Persian cats in this shed and they were burned to death; they were quite expensive cats. After that the local station master said to Robert Nickells, the farmer I was working for, 'It's those two girls you've got on your farm, one half-Italian and one half-German – they're spies.' He was quite sure.

23 JULY The Local Defence Volunteers, raised as an auxiliary force to combat a German invasion, is renamed the Home Guard

1 AUGUST Hitler updates his plans for Operation Sealion, the Invasion of England, in Directive 17, with a target date of 19-26 September; he orders the 'destruction of the RAF and the British aircraft industry'

1940

WAAFs at work in the Operations Room of 10 Group, Box, Colerne. (IWM: CH 13680)

A scene in bomb-damaged Liverpool, following an air raid by eight or nine German planes, October 1941. (IWM: PL 7410 B)

Harvest time: land girls reap the wheat on the Sussex Downs, August 1941. (IWM: HU 36274)

As a plotter **Anne Duncan** was based at one of the RAF's frontline fighter stations, at Hornchurch. As the Luftwaffe lost the Battle of Britain, the Blitz, night-time raids on the cities and towns of Britain, began. The air base was not ignored.

> We didn't awfully like going into the shelters, because they were not really bomb proof and if a bomb landed right on one it'd leave a very nasty mess. So what we usually did was to go outside and look and see what was going on. You could see the aeroplanes overhead; you could hear them all the time. There was this special droning noise. And then one night they started dropping bombs all around us. We all lay flat. There were lots dropped on the airfield. It was very exciting. This happened night after night, so you didn't get a lot of sleep during certain periods when they were having a particular drive at London. We were right in the pathway.

1940

13 AUGUST Following a brief delay caused by bad weather, the first major action of the Battle of Britain takes place, inaugurating weeks of heavy daylight raids by Luftwaffe bombers escorted by fighters

18 AUGUST The first Luftwaffe aircraft is brought down over London; German bombers successfully hit and damage RAF stations, though 71 Luftwaffe aircraft are lost in the raids

The ambition of Liverpudlian **Dorothy Hont** was to be a land girl, but in spring 1941 the sixteen-year-old was a witness to the Merseyside 'May Week' when waves of bombers hit the conurbation.

It was night after night after night. Your life rotated around the sirens. You'd go to work and you'd close the shop early or come home a little bit earlier, have a fast tea, get yourself into something warm, gather little bits of specials that you wanted to save, down to the shelter and that was it. And we used to knit in the shelter or play cards or guessing games or just doze. Half the time you were up to your ankles in water because water used to seep in. Every day you'd have to go down and bale out. So we used to put bricks on the floor to put our feet on, cold and miserable and horrible. I wouldn't wish it on anybody.

20 AUGUST Churchill broadcasts his inspirational tribute to the RAF pilots fighting the Battle of Britain: 'Never in the field of human conflict was so much owed by so many to so few'

15 SEPTEMBER The RAF scrambles all its fighters for the first time. 56 German aircraft are downed for 26 British losses, signalling the Luftwaffe's failure to gain air supremacy; today, this date is celebrated in the UK as 'Battle of Britain Day'

1940

CHAPTER ELEVEN

HOME FRONT

BY 1940 RATION BOOKS WERE PART OF EVERY household's life. In June 1939 the Women's Land Army had been reformed. And it was to be a far larger organization – with 80,000 members by 1944 – than it had been in between 1915 and 1918. The successes of the German U-boats in the Battle of the Atlantic meant that agricultural production had to rise. But initially, at Penhill Farm in Kent, **Vera Holdstock** did not get an enthusiastic reception.

They were very suspicious. We weren't local, they thought we must all be 'fast', and they did resent the fact that we were earning the same money as men, which is quite understandable. But gradually, as the war went on, we were accepted, when so many different people came to Tenterden. It got that the farmers just had to employ the girls because they were short of workers. Some men had joined up voluntarily, and some did remain, and gradually, when they saw how useful the girls were and how plucky they were, they were accepted and they really were very useful.

The only job that I did find unbearable was in the middle of winter: after we'd harvested the potatoes, they were put in big clamps, and at Penhill, in the winter – say in January and February – when

Women queue for their precious fish ration at the local fish shop in a painting by Evelyn Dunbar. (IWM: LD 3987)

The way it was supposed to be: the joys of the Land Army's harvest in a British propaganda picture. (IWM: HU 36273)

Instead of clumsy lectures, advertising put humour into Home Front campaigns. (IWM: PST 0630)

H.HILL & SON
ESTABLISHED OVER 50 YEARS
DEALERS IN GAME
MONGERS :: POULTERERS
FRESH FISH FROM THE COAST DAILY 9

WASTE THE FOOD
AND
HELP THE HUN

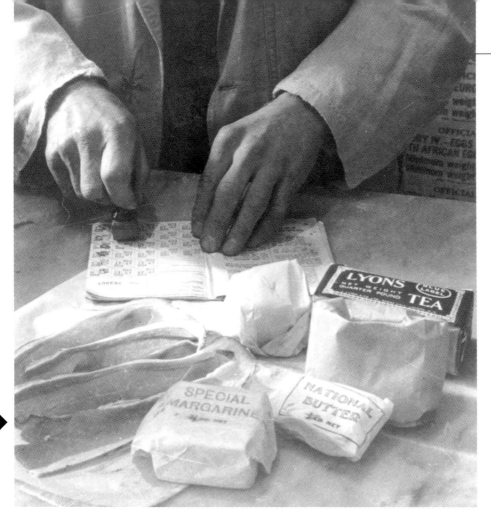

A shopkeeper marks a ration book. The books were unpopular, but kept the nation fed, clothed and healthy. (IWM: D 2373)

Imports of bananas virtually ceased during the war, but this stall, perhaps with a little help from the Ministry of Information, seems well stocked in contrast to the dearth of fresh fruit in Catherine Niblock's Glasgow. (IWM: HU 63736)

they started opening the clamps, we used to go out into an open field where these clamps were and we used to have to wash the mud off the potatoes in cold water, and it really was unbearably cold. But all the jobs I was given, I was able to tackle.

Rations varied according to fluctuations in the fortunes of war. The dark days of 1941, before large-scale American supplies had arrived, and when the U-boats were carving into the Atlantic convoys were the worst. Yet rationing had its virtues. Thanks to advice from nutritionists, diets improved, free or cheap milk was made available to

mothers and children. Infant mortality fell, as did the incidence of a scourge of pre-war life – tuberculosis. In 1944 twenty-year-old Glaswegian **Catherine Niblock** had given up working in a grocery and was working in a factory.

It was two ounces of tea, sugar, butter, margarine; you were allowed a quarter of ham, one egg a week, and everybody had the same standard in the ration book and that was it. So I had two ration books, for my father, and my own. So that was your basic – you'd have a quarter-pound of fat – that was two ounces for each adult – and half a pound of bacon, half a pound of sugar each. So that was our basic. But the manageress

21 SEPTEMBER Though civilians have been using London Underground stations as shelters since the bombing raids began, the British government grants permission officially for this practice to continue

30 SEPTEMBER The Luftwaffe delivers a final daylight raid on England, losing 47 aircraft to the RAF's 20. During September London has been bombarded with over 6,000 tons of high explosive bombs and 8,500 tons of incendiaries

of the shop I used to work in – that's where I used to leave my ration books because that's where I shopped – she was very good. She would on odd times accidentally have two chipped eggs – well, they were precious. The shell would have a slight chip. If somebody was coming in to get their three or four eggs, if they'd four books, they didn't want to take one with a chip on it, so you were allowed for breakages and spillages, so invariably my old boss used to keep me two aside because she knew how hard I had it. Fish and chip shops, they were open only maybe once or twice a week. So you were lucky if you could get some chips; something like that you were really lucky.

Between 1939 and 1944 consumption of fruit had fallen by more than 40 per cent, and of citrus fruit by 50 per cent.

Fruit – that was unheard of. I believe they did better in the south of England, because of the fruit crop there, but unless you knew someone who had a wee plot who grew things – I didn't have anybody that could give you an odd cabbage. I had no fruit during the war. And very, very little fresh vegetables.

In 1942, when she was still working at the local grocery, and living at home with her father, a steelworks labourer who drank, Catherine Niblock had a simple ambition.

1 OCTOBER The fourth phase of the Battle of Britain is characterized by the Luftwaffe's series of night-time raids known as the 'Blitz', which puts a far greater strain on British ground defences and civil-defence measures than the daylight raids

12 OCTOBER Hitler's planned invasion of England, Operation Sealion, is postponed until the spring of 1941

1940

I wanted to go into the services to get away. I'd no great ideas of serving my country. It was pretty selfish. At that age you don't have any great idealism. So I'd gone down to the Labour Exchange and made enquiries and I'd found out that I couldn't leave home without my father's permission. And even after I became eighteen, I was still not allowed because I was my father's sole female, without having a mother at home, I was kept.

But there was a shortage of labour. In December 1941 the industrial conscription of women was announced. It was the first time that any such measure had been taken anywhere in the world. Thus did the call-up arrive for Catherine from the Women's National Industrial Service. After training, she had a job at Cockburns, a factory producing safety valves for ships.

It would amaze you how one job gives you the feel for another job. If you're cutting something to a very fine – say ham – on a ham machine, where you get a feel for that, you still had a feel for the delicate balance of a weighing machine. You weren't aware

of it at the time, but I suppose all these things relate – you knew how delicate – if you'd a heavy hand obviously you would make a mistake with any machine you were using. So I think my grocery training must have helped me in the engineering part of it. I never thought I would be able to do it. Obviously that belies this feeling that boys used to be five years to serve their apprenticeship and here were women doing it in thirteen or twenty weeks.

Catherine was one of seven and a half million working women. Their male colleagues were invariably paid more and could see women as cheap competition, and as a corrosive force on trade unionism. Some unions tried to shut women out, but one by one they succumbed. Women couldn't be beaten, they should be joined.

The first thing I'd ever known about trade unions was when this gentleman came up – there were four girls in our section and he said, 'Would you like to join the trade union?'

I said, 'Oh, we don't want to join a trade union,' and everybody agreed. What would we do with a trade union? We were only in there temporary until

Women aged twenty-one or over register for the industrial call-up at Westminster Labour Exchange in 1941. (IWM: CP 5667 A)

1940

14 NOVEMBER Coventry is devastated during a 10-hour attack by the Luftwaffe, resulting in 500 deaths and 865 casualties, and the destruction of the city's medieval cathedral

3 DECEMBER Christmas rations are announced by the Food Minister: 4 oz. of sugar and 2 oz. of tea per person per week

A woman works on the
construction of a
Mosquito fighter-
bomber.
(IWM: TR 930)

The sea shall not have
them: women producing
life-saving rubber dinghies.

6 FEBRUARY The government publishes an official recipe for 'Blitz Broth'; there are to be many such 'austerity' recipes from the Ministry of Food, including 'Woolton Pie', a vegetarian dish named after Lord Woolton, Minister of Food from 1940

17 MARCH Ernest Bevin, Minister of Labour, announces a plan to mobilize masses of women to perform essential jobs in industry and the auxiliary services, especially in round-the-clock shell-filling factories

the war was finished and we'd no doubt in our mind that we would win the war and that would be our lives finished there and we would go back to whatever we were doing before. But then this chap came up and said, 'If you were in a trade union you would be paid bonuses for doing that job quicker.'

I said, 'Well, no one's told us that. You're the first person to mention it.'

And when he suggested we join the trade union – which was threepence a week, and we would qualify for a bonus – the four of us talked about it, and we had a wee discussion and some of us was really in favour of it, but we didn't really understand it. But eventually he explained how the trade union movement, before the war had started, were trying to get shorter working weeks for engineering and not to work on a Saturday.

Their ideal then was to get a forty-hour working week and stop this overtime and stop Saturday working and how you could get a bonus if you did

the job quicker.

Well, we had been working quite quickly. We knew the job was needed, we just automatically did it as quickly as we could. But eventually the four of us did join, and we did get a bonus. It was only a few shillings, it was hardly even worth bothering about. But we weren't really bothered about trade unions. We didn't know enough about it.

Not all women accepted industrial conscription. There were far more conscientious objectors in the Second World War than in the First, and they were generally far better treated by the authorities. In July 1942, twenty-one-year-old **Kathleen Wigham** was summonsed for refusing conscription and fined £5, which she would not pay. Kathleen was an absolutist, religious pacifist – she wouldn't do hospital work, which would release others to do

10 MAY The final heavy mission of the Battle of Britain: 550 Luftwaffe aircraft attack London with high-explosive and incendiaries, starting many fires and killing some 1,400 civilians; 27 German aircraft are lost. Since July 1940, the UK has endured more than 50,000 tons of bombs and still stands firm – heralding a significant change to German fortunes

military service. She was then working in the Herbal and Health Food Stores in Blackburn. The magistrates tried to persuade her to pay up, she refused, and she refused to allow her employer to pay the fine. The chairman of the magistrates told her she would be released at any time she agreed to pay the fine, and sentenced her to a minimum fourteen days in Strangeways. En route to the prison the police tried to dissuade her, 'You're too sensitive,' they said. 'It'll break you.' Conditions were grim.

This was at the time when Liverpool was being badly bombed each evening – Liverpool and Manchester; all the dock areas – and at night when you'd finished your work in the workshop – mine was sewing mailbags – you came back and at four o'clock you were back in your cell for tea and eight o'clock it was lights out, so there was obviously nothing to do, only to lie down, whether you went to sleep or not. And you virtually just stared up at the window, and everything was in darkness because of the blackout. You'd hear the sirens going, and hear gunfire and bombs dropping, and then this would

Women at work in a munitions factory in North Wales.
(IWM: CH 7328)

A former domestic servant operates an electric welding machine at a Southern Railway workshop.
(IWM: HU 36251)

24 MAY The world's most powerful battle cruiser, HMS *Hood*, is sunk by Germany's 45,000-ton battleship *Bismarck* which Germany claims is unsinkable. The *Bismarck* sunk by the Royal Navy on the 27th after a four-day pursuit

2 JUNE With the introduction of coupons for clothing, shop windows have to display a sign telling how many coupons are required to pay for items of clothing, in addition to the cost of the article

1941

The city of Manchester is hit during an air raid in January 1941.
(IWM: ZZZ 8139C)

The Salvation Army HQ in London collapses during the Blitz in May 1941.
(IWM: HU 650)

Areas of Liverpool are severely damaged during several devastating air raids in February 1942.
(IWM: KY 813 C)

22 JUNE Operation Barbarossa begins without any formal declaration of war, as German forces enter the Soviet Union in a surprise invasion

4 JULY Coal rationing introduced

14 AUGUST Churchill and US President Roosevelt hold a secret meeting and confirm a Western alliance with the signing of the Atlantic Charter

aggravate the girls, there would be terrible tension. You'd hear a girl shouting on the landing, 'Let me out! Let me out! Take us to the air raid shelters.' And nothing, no nothing happened, you'd hear no comforting voices. No one saying, 'Shut up,' to let you know there was someone about, and it just gave the impression that all the officers and wardresses must have gone to their safety shelters and we were just left.

Sometimes I would shout and say, 'We'll be all right, we're being watched over' – try to say a sentence, but you were very often sworn at back. It stopped you from even saying a prayer for them because they would tell you to 'B off' and the language was pretty foul really.

So I just said my own prayers and tried to sleep. But it was just hysteria. I was told the next morning with talking to one of the wardresses that you're not let out, they don't take the girls, they don't evacuate the building unless there's a bomb very close to the prison. Otherwise you're just left.

She served the fourteen days. Since the authorities realized that directing her to the Blackburn health food stores would result in her refusing to go there, they granted her 'unconditional exemption from any war work of any description'.

After the spring of 1941 the raids had ebbed, but they continued, even as British and American raids on Germany reached an unprecedented intensity. **Dorothy Hont**:

In the very bad times, such as the week of a bright moon or early dark nights you would have the sirens practically every night. And then if you went a few days without, that was as nerve-racking as the others because you were waiting for them. But after we had a bit of a respite you tended to get a little bit cheeky. You'd go to the pictures or something like that. I went to two dances and one cinema during the whole session of the war. That was the extent of my social life.

17 SEPTEMBER The government orders that potatoes will be sold at 1d (less than 1/2 p.) per pound to encourage people to eat more of them

2 DECEMBER All single women aged between 20 and 30 to be called up to join anti-aircraft crews or take over desk jobs vacated by conscripted men; the registration for service of single and married women up to the age of 40 will also begin

1941

American patrol: a US Infantryman jives with a WAAF at a 1943 dance. (IWM: HU 55852)

In the mood? US soldiers and British ATS turn a gymnasium into a dance hall in 1943. (IWM: HU 55851)

Nancy Bazin was commissioned and posted to an anti-aircraft gun unit, in a field near Bristol.

It was an extraordinary life. The women, in the ranks and as officers, were mainly in their early twenties, largely because that was considered the age at which they had the speed and the skills required, and the flexibility. The men were mainly in their thirties, and were those that had not been taken in the first flush of sending people overseas. That led to all sorts of problems which one would expect, emotional problems, because a lot of them were men of the world, attractive people, very often married, and there was a great deal of that kind of problem that arose from people becoming very involved. Some were very deep love affairs which lasted and turned into marriage, perhaps led to divorces which subsequently became happy marriages later after partners had parted and new marriages had been made. It was a fascinating period for study of people. There wasn't very much

to do and what entertainment there was you made within your own battery so you had little dances in your drill hall or your local NAAFI.

On the morning of my twenty-first birthday I was in the mess early, I suppose it was breakfast time, and someone arrived with a great bouquet of flowers. They knocked on the door and it was a sergeant and with him there were about fifty of the men and women and here they were equally men and women, my command was of men as much as women. We had this group outside and they were all singing: 'You are my sunshine.' This was the theme song, which they kept up through the day. Then, unknown to me, they planned this marvellous party in the evening where they had decorated the hall and done it all with electric light bulbs, twenty-one, and the cook had baked a great twenty-first birthday cake and unknown to me the brigadier and all the senior officers and everybody came down and we had a dance and we had the most marvellous twenty-first birthday party.

7 DECEMBER Taking the defences completely by surprise, the Japanese bomb Pearl Harbor, Hawaii, which leads to the declaration of war on Japan by the US. Britain and other Allied nations also declare war on Japan a day later

11 DECEMBER Hitler declares war on the United States; in response the US announces its own declarations of war against Germany and Italy

The skills of the girls had to be constantly trained, everything demanded the speed with which they could read out from the gun data tables and give you a height and give you all the things that you required — height, range — which they got from this gun data table book, great big heavy book. And they sat in the command post beside you. You had a Cartesian ground plan, which was like a big table with a map on it. But the map showed the immediate environment of the area you were looking after — well, say ten square miles. Under the table travelled a light which was moved directly in conjunction with all those pieces of information, mechanically moved. And you, the TCO, were calculating the point at which you decided that the right moment would be to fire, and therefore when it came within the range of your guns. So you were watching this all the time, and when you spotted that now you were within an inch, or whatever it was, you would call out over your intercom to the GPO: 'Fire!' and then within seconds you'd hear him repeat, 'Fire!' And the next moment you'd hear the guns.

2 FEBRUARY 2 million more British children receive free cod-liver oil

3 FEBRUARY The government restricts clothes prices, limiting the cost of a suit to £4 18s 8d (£4.92)

18 FEBRUARY It is reported that due to the shortage of cosmetics women are using cooked beetroot juice for lipstick, soot for eye make-up; gravy browning 'paint' is being applied as a substitute for silk stockings, accompanied by pencilled-in seams

CHAPTER TWELVE

THE FAR HORIZONS

IN 1940, WHILE ON LEAVE FROM THE RAF, THE
husband of **Yvonne Cormeau** was killed in
a London air raid. With her child at school,
she joined the WAAF and went to a
Lincolnshire RAF bomber station. Born in
China, educated in Brussels and Edinburgh,
Cormeau was bilingual in French and
English, and also spoke Spanish and
German. She was a natural recruit for the
Special Operations Executive, with its

network of agents across Europe. She had
assumed she would go into unoccupied Vichy
France, but by the time of the drop Vichy
France, led by collaborationist Marshal
Pétain, had been occupied by the Germans.
They gave us some ideas about living and operating

WAAF personnel occupy a radiolocation detection post.
(IWM: C 1868)

A female pilot of the Air Transport Auxiliary prepares for a flight.

119

Allied women pilots of the Air Transport Auxiliary.
(IWM: CH 8945)

in France but they said, 'You've got to judge. When you're on the spot things might change. All we can tell you is there may be certain days of the week when you can't have certain drinks or foods in certain cafés, so don't ask. Just try and look out and see what is on the menu and advertised for those days. Please don't do too much dying of your hair or have very noticeable make-up or things like that because you'll fall foul at some time or other. Try and dress as they do locally as much as possible. If you're going to live in the country, don't have manicure.'

In 1943, after training, the day came when she was to drop into France, for the SOE's F Section, as an agent and wireless operator.

On a Sunday afternoon I was taken to a house not far from the airfield and given a wonderful meal. I thought at the time it was the condemned man's last meal. I was taken over to the field to be dressed up in my jump suit. Then I went into the aircraft and said good evening to the crew who had lined up each side

of the hold over which I had to climb. We took off in a beautiful sunset in England.

At one moment I was given a nice hot drink by the despatcher and then I saw he opened a hole in the floor of the fuselage. He came and attached my silk cord to the side of the aircraft and told me to get ready in my thoughts. Also at that moment I could see the red light coming on and I knew when the green light came on and the despatcher gave me a sign, I had to fly through the hole. This happened. I went down very well indeed. The slipstream from the motors carried me off. Slowly but surely my parachute opened out on its own and I didn't even feel the jerk on my shoulder. When I got away from the slipstream my legs slowly went down and I could see the ground. I only had a handbag with money in strapped behind my back, filling in a way the lower

1942

11 MARCH The government announces a ban on the baking of white bread

14 MAY Newly included in women's war fashions are 'bare legs for patriotism'

30 MAY Air Marshal Harris orders a major raid on Cologne involving more than 1,000 aircraft. 2,000 tons of bombs are dropped for a total loss of only 40 aircraft; RAF chiefs claim to have destroyed more than 200 factories

A gathering of a French resistance group, not unlike the resistance network that Yvonne Cormeau joined in the Gironde region of southern France.

vertebrae of the spine so that the shock wouldn't damage anything. I was dressed in what I thought was normal for France, a black coat and skirt and silk blouse – and that went very well indeed – and black shoes. My ankles were bandaged because I was in shoes and not jump boots.

She had been parachuted into the Gironde department of southern France, and became part of a local resistance SOE network known as the 'Wheelwright circuit'.

I left my wedding and engagement ring in England but one very observant woman told me about three months after I got there,

'You're married, aren't you? There's a shiny line on your finger!' You never knew whether a man or

woman was willing to give information to the Gestapo. Sometimes it was a personal vendetta between two families but of course repercussions could be much worse. Other times it was for money, which was serious.

The Germans were tracing her transmissions. And Gestapo money bought an unexpected informer.

By 1944 the Gestapo had got it down. They found someone willing to talk, a Spaniard, one of the Communist Spaniards who had left Spain, running away from Franco. And he said, 'Yes – at the village of Castelnau there is an Englishwoman with a radio set.'

So the Germans started looking for someone in all those villages, because there were in one département eight Castelnaus. They all had a second-barrelled name. They were either on a river or a hill, or low or something like that. They never happened to come to the one where I did go back from time to time – quite often towards the end because this was such a

3 JUNE US ships and carrier-borne aircraft engage Japanese naval forces in the Battle of Midway, resulting in the withdrawal of the Japanese fleet, with heavy losses, four days later

21 JUNE Tobruk falls to Rommel's Afrika Korps, with the loss of more than 20,000 Allied prisoners

27 JULY Sweet rationing is introduced; it will stay in force in Britain until 1954

Photographed in 1944, Air Vice Marshal J. H. Broadhurst, DSO., DFC., AFC, Anne Duncan's station commander in 1942. (IWM: CH 13093)

British women aviators may not have flown combat missions but, like Anne Duncan, they were no strangers to Spitfires.

hamlet, there was no electricity, no running water, just one well. And in their methodic way, they'd decided no Englishwoman would live in such conditions.

Yvonne Cormeau had several close encounters, but was never captured.

By 1942 **Anne Duncan** had risen in the WAAF from Aircraftwoman 2 grade – an 'ACW Plonk' – through ACW1 to a commission as a cipher officer. But she wanted to use the skill she had gained just before the war, to fly. In the Soviet Union there were women fighter pilots. In Britain there were ferry pilots, women – and men – of the Air Transport Auxiliary. Their job was to fetch new aeroplanes from the factories and fly them to maintenance units, and then fly them on to squadron delivery. Backed by her station commander, Group Captain – later Air Chief

19 AUGUST Almost 6,000 troops, mostly Canadians, take part in the disastrous raid on Dieppe; the landing is completed, but very few target installations are attacked for the loss of many lives and some 1,500 prisoners, besides aircraft, tanks and landing-craft

24 OCTOBER The second Battle of El Alamein begins when General Montgomery orders a 1,000-gun bombardment of the German positions and minefields, followed by a night attack

Marshal – Sir Harry Broadhurst, she was accepted by the ATA. It meant her quitting the WAAF, and taking on ATA training.

There were only about four or five women in my course as opposed to about fifteen or twenty men, and only about half that number came through. You did get turned down if you didn't make the grade – they were quite selective. After all, you were being trained for something quite important. You get up in one of those aeroplanes, they cost a great deal of money. *If you are going to break them up you're not worth having. If you're going to cause trouble and get neurotic and nervous and start getting ill or something, they are much better off without you – better go off and do something else. This was the sort of thing they turned people down for. A lot of people didn't find they could find their way. I was always very practical and I didn't have any trouble at all. I used to be able to map read and can do to this day with the greatest of ease.*

25 OCTOBER The milk ration is reduced to two and a half pints per person per week

3 NOVEMBER Montgomery successfully breaks through the Afrika Korps' front line at El Alamein

17 JANUARY For the first time since May 1941, London is subjected to a night-time raid by German bombers, totalling 118 aircraft

1943

Evelyn White was a nurse from Birmingham who had worked through the London Blitz in the Mile End Hospital. Deeply impressed by the pacifists of the Quaker Friends Ambulance Unit, she decided to join them. In June 1943, the twenty-one-year-old made the perilous flight from India, over the 'Hump' into Nationalist-controlled China. Soon after her arrival, while based in Baoshan, a Chinese troop train was derailed nearby.

It was a revelation to me, in spite of being in the Blitz in London. That was comparatively civilized, because we all had the facilities, the hospital wards, the blood plasma, the civil defence, the Fire Brigade. We had a back-up of wonderful people, air raid wardens, and all the facilities, buses and ambulances to transport.

Here, in the wilderness, where there were no ambulances, no back-up, no blood plasma, very few medicines that we needed, or splints – it was improvisation. They were lucky to survive. I don't know what would have happened if we hadn't been there.

Women of the Air Transport Auxiliary's No 5 Ferry Pilots Pool, based at Hatfield, Hertfordshire.

5 MARCH The Krupp munitions factory at Essen is raided by aircraft from RAF Bomber Command comprising Lancaster, Halifax, Stirling and Wellington bombers, marking the start of regular action against Germany's industrial centre, the Ruhr Valley

17 MAY RAF Lancaster bombers carry out the 'Dambusters' raid, bombing and partly destroying two major dams, the Möhne and Eder, and causing considerable damage within Germany's industrial heartland

Disaster waiting to happen. A Walrus (Supermarine) aeroplane, of the type in which Anne Duncan had a near-fatal crash on the Isle of Wight. (IWM: CH 18540)

Anne Duncan flew everything from light planes through Spitfires to medium bombers and transport aircraft like the Douglas DC3 Dakota. Close to the end of the war, at Cowes on the Isle of Wight, an encounter with an amphibious Walrus was not a success.

The Walrus was a very unattractive aeroplane to fly. It was like several sacks of coal. It was terribly unstable and wallowed and it made the most dreadful noise. It was a nasty airfield on slope. You usually had to take off slightly uphill on a slope and as a Walrus was a very lumbering kind of aeroplane I took off this day very much across wind, couldn't get an angle into the wind. As soon as I'd opened up, and we'd left the ground it felt to me as though it wanted to turn over on to its back. I simply couldn't hold it. I concluded that the controls must have been crossed, something which could happen, had happened, so I throttled back. But the minute I throttled back, it righted itself so then I quickly realized that it wasn't the controls, it must be able to take off, but by this time, since I'd left the ground, we'd swung even further across the wind.

It was a silly thing probably in retrospect to have opened up again but I did. I thought I could make it but it was clearly not going to be so. I didn't want to crash into a hangar so I managed to steer clear. I had throttled back again by this time, I could see I was going to crash. Anyway we hit a little shed at the side of the airfield. That's the last thing I remember, the aeroplane tipping forwards. I landed apparently alongside, over a little road, and alongside a bungalow, which was just on the other side of the road.

I think one of the wings actually hit it but it so happened that, luckily, that day – which was quite illegal – I was not strapped in. In this particular aeroplane you couldn't reach the pedals properly, so that if you were strapped in you were even less able to lean forward and reach the pedals. I had rather short legs. So I left myself unstrapped in. When it landed it burst into flames immediately but I was half thrown out of the cockpit. The baker's man was just delivering his bread at that particular moment. He had to dive a bit to get out of the way but once he saw what had happened he came rushing along. He pulled me out of the flames. I was burnt, my clothes were burnt. I was quite unconscious – but he managed to pull me clear.

Vera Lynn was world famous, Anne Shelton almost as popular; reactions from service personnel to the Entertainments National

12 JULY Battle of Kursk: Soviet forces defeat a German army in greatest tank battle ever fought; first overwhelming defeat for Hitler's Panzers

15 AUGUST Allied forces invade the Italian mainland

8 SEPTEMBER Italy's unconditional surrender and armistice with the Allies is announced.

28 NOVEMBER Churchill, Roosevelt and Stalin meet in Tehran to discuss the defeat of Germany

1943

Service Association – ENSA – frontline performances ranged from enthusiastic to concurrence with ENSA's alternative title, 'Every Night Something Awful'. **Evelyn**

White encountered the Chinese Army's equivalent in Kutsing.

We were at a party where a group of actors who were producing the classic Chinese play 'Lady

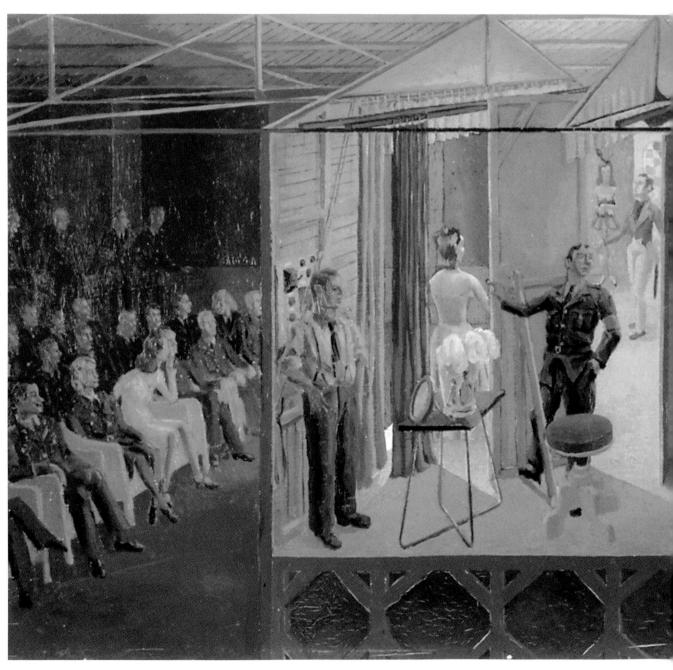

21 JANUARY Hitler orders retaliatory raids against London and Southern England; only 96 out of 270 aircraft reach their targets, and some are brought down. In contrast, almost 700 RAF bombers make successful raids on Berlin, Kiel and Magdeburg

18 APRIL In the heaviest Allied air raid of the war over 2,000 bombers drop more than 4,000 tons of bombs on Germany. Meanwhile, the last of the Operation Steinbeck raids on London occurs, with an attack on the capital by more than 100 bombers

Precious Stream', in Mandarin came round. The actors appeared in the most magnificent costumes, very old some of them. That was fine but the awful thing was that the men played the ladies' parts.

When they started singing in the high-pitched strangulated voices and we had to listen to this for four hours, that wasn't so good. As you probably know, the musical instrument, the Chinese violin, only

Painted by Frank Graves, members of the Entertainments National Services Association (ENSA) put on a show in a NAAFI canteen hut. (IWM: ART LD 1690)

6 JUNE D-Day landings – Allied troops invade Europe, storming the beaches of Normandy, France

13 JUNE The first V-1 flying bombs are launched at England from the Pas-de-Calais; only 4 out of 10 V-1s cross the English Channel successfully, but 6 people are killed in Bethnal Green, London

1944

has three strings. It sounds very odd to the western ear and slightly off-key.

We sat back and thought, 'We must be polite and enjoy it.' It was rather nice to be in on this wonderful play. I'd heard a lot about it but of course didn't know. The audience were very appreciative. All the Chinese Army seemed to spend most of the performance eating sunflower seeds — wise of them, it's full of vitamin N; I think we give it to our birds — that was fine, but what they would do was crack the seed between their teeth and spit out

the casings to the four winds — if you happened to be in the way that was just too bad.

Nan Kenway had found other work after the collapse of the Newquay concert party back in 1939. By the end of the war, with her husband and partner Douglas Young, working with ENSA, she had performed in Italy, North Africa, France, Belgium, Holland, India — and Burma.

After we left the Irrawaddy at Katha — that was in

6 JULY Churchill informs Parliament that 2,752 civilians have been killed as a result of attacks by 3,745 V-1 flying bombs

11 JULY Over a million children are evacuated from London to safer rural areas following the mass destruction caused by the V-1 bombs

25 AUGUST Paris is liberated by Allied troops

Burma – the General said we were to have been sent back. And we said, 'Oh, please, we want to go forward where there's no entertainment at all.' It was only just Dougie and me. So the General very kindly said, well, if I had sufficient coverage, we could go.

We had two jeeps. I sat in the front jeep; two soldiers, rifles at the ready. Dougie sat in the back jeep with the piano, which kept falling off. I can't tell you what the roads were like. And forward we went for nearly a hundred miles.

And there were no white women at all. There were no nurses, nothing. Was I a success? Oh, happy days! And they got together, and they ran up a tent. And it was as easy as that. There were all these lovely silk parachutes coming down with supplies. And there was the tent. And it was quite easy to find supports – they were out in the jungle, plenty of uprights, loads of bamboo; and plenty of rope from the parachutes. And before you could say Jack Robinson, we had a tent. And then they got together and thought, 'Oh yes, she'll want to go somewhere.' So they went a little bit further away. And when I went along, you could have heard me laughing in Calcutta. They had dug a lovely new hole. And they'd got a Tate's sugar box. And they'd cut out just the right size. Well they knew the size – they'd been following me round the camp all day, you see. And when I went in, it was upholstered with grass and white silk parachute. I've never had a padded loo since, or before.

In a concert organized by ENSA in November 1940 George Formby entertains 2,000 people in underground shelters. (IWM: HU 36154)

British troops enjoy a sing-song round a piano at a party organized by ENSA.

27 AUGUST RAF Bomber Command launches its first major daylight bombing raid on Germany since the early war months; since 1942, the USAAF has carried out daylight strategic raids, with the RAF bombing by night

8 SEPTEMBER The first V-2 rocket lands in Chiswick, London, killing three and injuring ten; fired from a mobile launcher in the German-occupied suburb of The Hague, the rocket's 192-mile journey takes only 5 minutes

1944

CHAPTER THIRTEEN

VICTORY

ON 6 JUNE 1944 ALLIED ARMIES LANDED IN Normandy. That winter the German army in the west lost in its last offensive, the 'Battle of the Bulge'. It took place in Belgium, 'the gallant little Belgium' whose invasion by the Germans thirty years earlier had first led Britain into twentieth-century European war. By March 1945 attacks by V-1 'Doodlebug' and V-2 rockets on England ceased; the skies of Britain were at peace.

On 7 May the Germans unconditionally surrendered. A day later came VE Day, the official end of the war in Europe. Yet for women and men in Britain there was another source of anxiety – the war in the Far East against Japan, which was expected to go on into 1946.

On 6 August the Japanese city of Hiroshima became the first target of an atomic attack; 80,000 people died in the raid. Nagasaki was atom bombed on 9 August;

Allied troops land in Normandy.

The future past? Hiroshima in the aftermath of the atomic bomb. (IWM: MH 29447)

40,000 people died. After her escape from France in 1940 **Josephine Pearce**, had worked the North Africa and the Near East, with a frontline surgical unit, and later joined the Women's Royal Navy Service, the Wrens. On VE Day she was based in Plymouth.

> I remember flinging myself at some burly man in the dockyard and kissing him on both cheeks in the proper, true, French way. And he heaving me up off the ground and whirling me round. Everybody went absolutely crazy.

Just outside Plymouth twenty-year-old land girl **Jean Evans**, who was working for the Timber Corps, headed for the city.

> I saw Henry V that afternoon, for the first time, in the Plymouth Odeon, and came out and had a meal, and in the evening, of course, we were all on Plymouth Hoe, dancing with the sailors. Everybody was over the moon. They had been bombed so dreadfully – Plymouth was in an awful state – but everybody was happy.

Just outside Coventry, another land girl, twenty-five-year-old **Margaret Couling**, was at Wall Hill farm.

> We celebrated. We had an enormous bonfire. We all went out and we sang and we had hot potatoes and we all put all the lights up. But I suppose in comparison with the jollifications in the big cities, we were reasonably quiet. We'd still got to go on and milk the cows and feed the animals. So we couldn't spend the whole day jollificating. It was a much more subdued enjoyment and the same with VJ Day.

We had a bonfire again to celebrate. But it was more muted, although everybody was relieved we could put the lights on, we could take the masks off cars. We could drive in complete freedom. The only scare we'd had as far as the Germans were concerned – we had one or two prisoners of war working locally. But they were all fairly amenable. Nobody caused any trouble.

In April 1945 the brother of **Dorothy Hont**, captured in France before Dunkirk, returned, emaciated and ill from a prison camp in eastern Germany. A few days later it was VE Day, and a street party.

We made sardine sandwiches and somebody brought a bit of cheese we grated. And various people who had boys in the navy and brought stuff

In celebration of VE Day a street tea party takes place in Islington.

for their mums, they opened up their hearts – we had this big do.

In Glasgow **Catherine Niblock** was out of the factory.

We had a bonfire in the street – I don't know where the wood came from. There was someone playing the recording, and we were out dancing in the streets, happy, so happy. Nearly every other street had a bonfire, lit up, because you didn't need the blackout. Everybody was happy about it.

16 DECEMBER In the Ardennes, the Battle of the Bulge, a last-ditch attempt by the Germans to divide the Allied thrust towards Germany, begins. Initially successful, it is eventually defeated by US forces, with British units and aircraft in support

4 FEBRUARY 1945 Yalta Conference – Churchill, Roosevelt and Stalin meet once again to discuss the world's post-war future

In London, more than half a decade on from Mickey Mouse gas masks and High Wycombe, **Sylvia Townson** was entered for a VE Day talent contest by her father.

I belted out 'You Are My Sunshine' and I came second – a boy came first. They had a bonfire in the middle of the road. The food just arrived from everywhere.

Three months later, she celebrated VJ Day in Mountain Ash, Wales – to which she had been evacuated and where she had gone to school, following the 1944–5 V-weapon Blitz on London.

That was a great day in the history of Mountain Ash. They had an enormous street party in Cilhaul Terrace. I don't know where all the tables came from but they had one long table almost the whole length of the terrace and masses and masses of

food and bunting and drink. And everybody participated. And the children had a fancy dress party, and because I'd just come from London I didn't have any fancy dress of my own. So this dear old mam, an eighty-year-old lady, dug into her wardrobe or her attic. And somewhere from her past – never quite decided how – she managed to produce a Japanese kimono that was absolutely beautiful, and wound that around me. She had a fan and parasol and those Japanese shoes, pieces of wood with ribbons attached, very difficult to walk in, and some artificial chrysanthemums. And I went along – it seems extraordinary, but there you are – celebrating the end of the war in Japan dressed as a Japanese lady. And I won the fancy dress.

The Thames is illuminated by floodlights and a firework display as VE Day celebrations continue into the night.

13-14 FEBRUARY The German city of Dresden is devastated, following night and day attacks by 750 RAF and 400 USAAF bombers. Some 100,000 people are killed, with another 300,000 injured, for the city is full of refugees

24 FEBRUARY 18-year-old Princess Elizabeth joins the ATS as 2nd Subaltern Elizabeth Alexandra Mary Windsor; she qualifies as a driver on 14 April, and is promoted to Junior Commander on 27 July

CHAPTER FOURTEEN

AFTERMATH

DOROTHY BING WAS A CONSCIENTIOUS OBJECTOR through the two wars.

Up to 1914 it was absolutely Victorian. We did the same things as the Victorians did; our homes looked like Victorian homes. And the war itself was such a complete upheaval that life wasn't the same again afterwards. It's true, more or less, of the Second World War too. When you think that in 1939 about a third of the people, really, were undernourished in this country, just had insufficient food to develop normally. This is a different world.

It was as if, in 1900, there had been a good fairy who granted wishes, but nobody had noticed that she had a companion in the shadows. There were campaigns for votes for women, an end to women's chattel status,

'Ruby Loftus screwing a breech-ring': Dame Laura Knight's 1943 portrait celebrates the dignity and skill of women workers and encapsulates the opportunities that war gave to women on the home front. (IWM: LD 2850)

134

decent education and housing, health and maternity care. As the century advanced, so did women, barriers fell, fields of employment opened up. Britain got a health service, better schools, maternity care, family allowances. Democracy and industrialization invaded everything. But emerging from the shadows, that companion provided the bill. In the First World War the British Empire lost more than 900,000 lives. In the Second World War 355,000 British citizens were killed. In the twentieth century some 100 million people worldwide died in wars, as nations

First World War women war workers – land girl, nurse and munitions worker – in Edmund Dulac's watercolour 'The Sisters'. (IWM: ART 2509)

Women campaigners demonstrate for their right to the vote. (IWM: Q 107102)

became armed camps, unarmed citizens targets and the divisions between soldiers, civilians, workers, men and women blurred. War had invaded everything. But women discovered they could do anything. **Ruby Ord**:

> WAACS were marvellous – at putting on a show, doing anything that was required of them. This is women, to my mind. They are most adaptable and they are so competent and capable in emergencies. We are a special generation. They had no training. Whatever they went to do, they were turned to as a

During the First and Second World Wars women proved they were capable of anything, whether they worked on the land, operated machinery in factories (right), joined one of the armed forces, or took on any type of employment from which they were previously excluded – nothing was beyond their capability.

7 MARCH US forces cross the Rhine into Germany by seizing intact the Ludendorff Bridge at Remagen

23 MARCH British and Canadian forces cross the Rhine, supported by airborne landings

27 MARCH The last V-2 rocket launched at the UK lands in Orpington, Kent; 2,754 civilians have been killed by V-2s, 6,523 have been seriously injured

29 MARCH The last V-1 flying bomb to land in the UK hits Kent; 6,184 civilians have been killed by V-1s, 17,981 seriously injured

15 APRIL British troops liberate the Bergen-Belsen concentration camp in north-eastern Germany. The Allied liberation of this and other concentration and extermination camps reveals the full extent of the Nazis' genocidal policies

1945

The future Queen, Princess Elizabeth, was enlisted for the war effort as a member of the Auxiliary Territorial Service (ATS). (IWM: TR 2835)

ATS women use an ID telescope at an anti-aircraft gunsite in 1942. (IWM: TR 468)

30 APRIL Adolf Hitler and his wife of one day, Eva Braun, commit suicide, she by poison, he by shooting. Their bodies are taken outside and burnt

8 MAY VE-Day: following Germany's official surrender on 7 May, Victory in Europe is celebrated throughout Britain; Churchill, King George VI and President Truman broadcast triumphant speeches

A member of the Women's Air Auxiliary Force (WAAF) checks an air-sea rescue boat in 1942. (IWM: TR 302)

last resort, so that they weren't prepared. But they did the job, it blew the gaffe that men were the superior sex, even in works and places like that, in munitions factories, everywhere women went they did awfully well.

By 1918 **Florence Farmborough** was out of Russia, and she did not return until the 1960s, the heyday of the Soviet Union.

These women that I knew in those days – there were hundreds and hundreds of them, completely illiterate, completely unenlightened, completely away from the real life of the world. And they could manage with a vernacular of probably two hundred to three hundred words at the most. When I went to Russia twelve years ago these women were completely educated,

marvellously alert, with much wider ideas, enormously wide horizons because they had been educated. And education had completely transformed them. They were no longer poverty-stricken, benighted peasants in the country, but they were townswomen going to their offices, to their mills, to their factories, to their shops. A wonderful transformation. I have always known that education was essential.

After the Second World War **Evelyn White**, back from China, married a vicar.

People, whether they're Russian, Chinese, Japanese, Indian, American – we all have the same hopes and fears. We all want to live as long as God allows us to in peace, or comparative peace. We all want our children to grow up, we don't want our sons to be thrown into another war. There's something missing in our make-up or in our leadership or we've got the wrong leaders, which makes nations go to war or want to go to war. I don't know the answer. I wish I did.

6 AUGUST USAAF Boeing B-29 Superfortresses bomb Hiroshima. One aircraft, the *Enola Gay*, is carrying 'Fat Boy', the first atomic bomb to be dropped on enemy territory. 75 per cent of the city is devastated, and some 150,000 people die

9 AUGUST A second atomic bomb is dropped on Japan. In Nagasaki, a third of the city is destroyed; c. 75,000 people are killed or wounded. As with Hiroshima, many more will die over the years from the long-term effects of wounds and radiation

1945

For **Ruby Ord**, the patriot of 1914, her experiences, during and after the 1914–18 war changed everything.

> I hadn't very long been demobilized before I was a pacifist, sympathizing with the people who had the courage to refuse to fight, because they are the only people who will ever end war. I think women could have done this. Now, with nuclear war, I don't know what we could do.
>
> I am a thinker. I do not react emotionally. At my reunions, when I have to toast the forces, I feel very fed up about it. But I do it just to be amiable and not upset the applecart, because one of the women sitting there's got two sons in the navy. But they know my feelings. I didn't even want to wear uniform – I went out as a woman to help. They wanted women to help release men for the forces, and that was all, and that was all I did. But I was fanatically patriotic. Now I am a pacifist, so

After the first catastrophe: women of the Volunteer Aid Detachment march at a peace parade in London, July 1919.

In memory of the dead of the First World War, a two-minute silence is first observed in London on 11 November 1919.

> if my time came again I wouldn't do the same. I should say no, let us be strong, all of us, and refuse to fight. It is the only way to end war. As long as somebody will fight there will be war. It is no solution of anything. Until men are strong enough to resist fighting, nothing will ever be solved. I have lived so long, and it has been going on and on, and now it is worse. Because if you can kill millions of people without even having to see what you are doing, it is so much easier to do it, isn't it – press a button?

14 AUGUST Japan surrenders unconditionally. In 1946, under the US occupation of Japan, the Emperor Hirohito renounces his divine status in favour or ruling as a constitutional monarch

15 AUGUST VJ-Day ('Victory over Japan' Day) is celebrated throughout Britain and the USA, as well as in other countries that had fought in the Allied cause

1939-1945 THE COST: Great Britain lost 264,443 servicemen and women killed during the Second World War, with another 277,077 wounded and 213,919 captured or missing. In addition, 92,673 British civilians were killed, of which 30,248 died on service with the merchant marine, and 60,595 as a result of the Axis bombing – thousands of them women and children; 624 members of the women's auxiliary services were also killed

The Voices – list of contributors

Agnes Allan 000517/09
Nancy Bazin 9596
Dorothy Bing 555/9
Isabel Brown 000844
Margareta Burkill (née Braun) 004588/08
Mairi Chisholm of Chisholm 000771/04
Isabella Clarke (née McGee) 000774/04
Yvonne Cormeau 7369
Margaret Couling 009456
Jane Cox 000705/06
Brigitte Davies (née Jacobs) 004438
Anne Duncan 9995/4
Caroline Edgley 000515/05
Annie Edwards 000740/15
Edith Evans 000508/06
Jean Evans 8883
Florence Farmborough 000312/17
Antonia Gamwell 000502/11
Vera Holdstock 008847
Dorothy Hont 009527
Annie Howell 000613/08
Nan Kenway 10063/2
Elizabeth Lee (née Dowland) 000779/16
Mary Lees 000506/07
Elsie McIntyre (née Bateson) 000673
Lilian Miles 000854
Catherine Niblock 008301
Doris Nicholls 4634/6
Ruby Ord 44/5
Josephine Pearce 000831
Helen Pease (née Wedgwood) 821/20
Eleanora Pemberton 003188
Alice Remington 000511/08
Caroline Rennles (née Webb) 000566/07
Emily Rumbold (née Newing) 000576
Mary Rumney (née Collis) 000739/16
Sylvia Townson (née Limburg) 5417
Margaret Warren 00512/06
Evelyn White 10146/6
Kathleen Wigham (née Derbyshire) 004761/7

The numbers are IWM classifications.

Select Bibliography

These are among the books drawn on for *Women at War*. The dates refer to their first publication.

Arnold-Foster, Mark, *The World at War* (Collins, London, 1973)

Brittain, Vera, *Testament of Youth: An Autobiographical Study of the Years 1900–1925* (Victor Gollancz, 1933)

Calder, Angus, *The Myth of the Blitz* (Jonathan Cape, London. 1991)

Calder, Angus, *The People's War* (Jonathan Cape, London, 1960)

Ferguson, Niall, *The Pity of War* (Allen Lane, The Penguin Press, 1998)

Howard, Michael, *The Invention of Peace* (Profile Books, 2000)

Liddington, Jill, *The Long Road to Greenham: Feminism and Anti-Militarism in Britain Since 1820* (Virago, 1989)

Marlow, Joyce (Ed.), *The Virago Book of Women and the Great War* (Virago, 1998)

Purnell's History of the Second World War (1966)

Rowbotham, Sheila, *A Century of Women* (Viking, 1997)

Taylor, A. J. P., *The First World War: An Illustrated History* (Hamish Hamilton, 1963)

Taylor, A. J. P., *English History 1914–1945* (Oxford University Press, Oxford, 1965)

Woollacott, Angela, *On Her Their Lives Depend: Munitions Workers in the Great War* (University of California Press, 1994)

CD music credits and acknowledgements

Sound effects and 'Long Way To Tipperary' used courtesy of the Imperial War Museum Sound Archive.

Musical extracts used courtesy of River Records.

Will Oakland and Chorus: 'Just Before The Battle' – taken from *Your Country Needs You* (RRCD49/IWM)

F. Wheeler and Chorus: 'Here We Are, Here We Are' – taken from *Your Country Needs You* (RRCD49/IWM)

Carroll Gibbons: 'Fools Rush In' – taken from *Forces Romance* (RRCD35/IWM)

The Glenn Miller Orchestra: 'In The Mood' – taken from *Our Finest Hour* (RRCD03/IWM)

Band of H. M. Coldstream Guards: 'Keep The Home Fires Burning' – taken from *Your Country Needs You* (RRCD49/IWM)

Lew Stone and his band with Sam Browne: 'Till The Lights Of London Shine Again' – taken from *Who Do You Think You Are Kidding Mr Hitler?* (RRCD13)

All titles available from the Imperial War Museum (Tel: 020 7416 5000)

CD interviewees

Nancy Bazin
Isabel Brown
Isabella Clarke (née McGee)
Yvonne Cormeau
Jane Cox
Florence Farmborough
Vera Holdstock
Dorothy Hont
Nan Kenway
Elizabeth Lee (née Dowland)
Catherine Niblock
Ruby Ord
Josephine Pearce
Helen Pease (née Wedgwood)
Alice Remington
Caroline Rennles (née Webb)
Emily Rumbold (née Newing)
Sylvia Townson (née Limburg)
Margaret Warren
Evelyn White
Kathleen Wigham (née Derbyshire)